W9-BCG-515

GRAPHIC BIOGRAPHIES

GEORGE WASHINGTON

LEADING A NEW NATION

by Matt Doeden

illustrated by Cynthia Martin

Consultant:

Mary V. Thompson, Research Specialist

Mount Vernon Ladies' Association

Mount Vernon, Virginia

Capstone
press

Mankato, Minnesota

Graphic Library is published by Capstone Press,
151 Good Counsel Drive, P.O. Box 669, Mankato, Minnesota 56002.
www.capstonepress.com

Printed in the United States of America

1 2 3 4 5 6 10 09 08 07 06 05

Library of Congress Cataloging-in-Publication Data
Doeden, Matt.
George Washington: leading a new nation / by Matt Doeden; illustrated by Cynthia Martin
p. cm.—(Graphic library. Graphic biographies)
Includes bibliographical references and index.
ISBN 0-7368-4963-7 (hardcover)
1. Washington, George, 1732–1799—Juvenile literature. 2. Presidents—United States—Biography—Juvenile literature. I. Title. II. Series.
E312.66.D64 2006
973.4'1'092—dc22 2005006530

Summary: In graphic novel format, tells the life story of George Washington, the leader of the Continental army during the Revolutionary War and the first president of the United States.

Art and Editorial Direction
Jason Knudson and Blake A. Hoena

Designers
Jennifer Bergstrom and Jason Knudson

Editor
Donald Lemke

Editor's note: Direct quotations from primary sources are indicated by a yellow background.

Direct quotations appear on the following pages:
Pages 13, 17, from *George Washington: Anguish and Farewell (1793–1799)* by James Thomas Flexner (Boston: Little, Brown, 1972).
Page 26, from transcripts of Washington's Farewell Address, September 19, 1796. The Papers of George Washington (http://gwpapers.virginia.edu/documents/farewell/transcript.html).

TABLE OF CONTENTS

CHAPTER 1

YOUNG GEORGE WASHINGTON

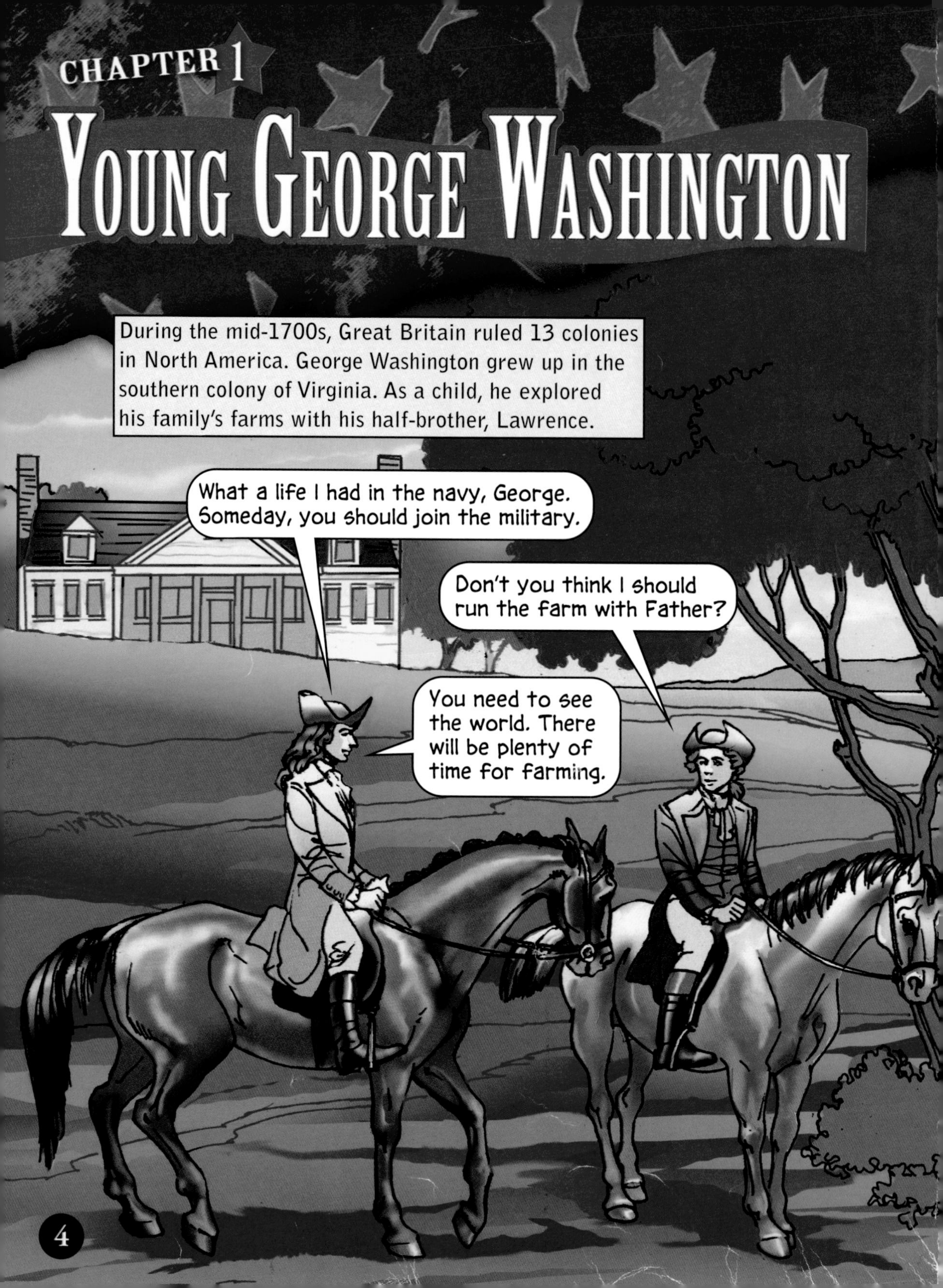
During the mid-1700s, Great Britain ruled 13 colonies in North America. George Washington grew up in the southern colony of Virginia. As a child, he explored his family's farms with his half-brother, Lawrence.
What a life I had in the navy, George. Someday, you should join the military.
Don't you think I should run the farm with Father?
You need to see the world. There will be plenty of time for farming.

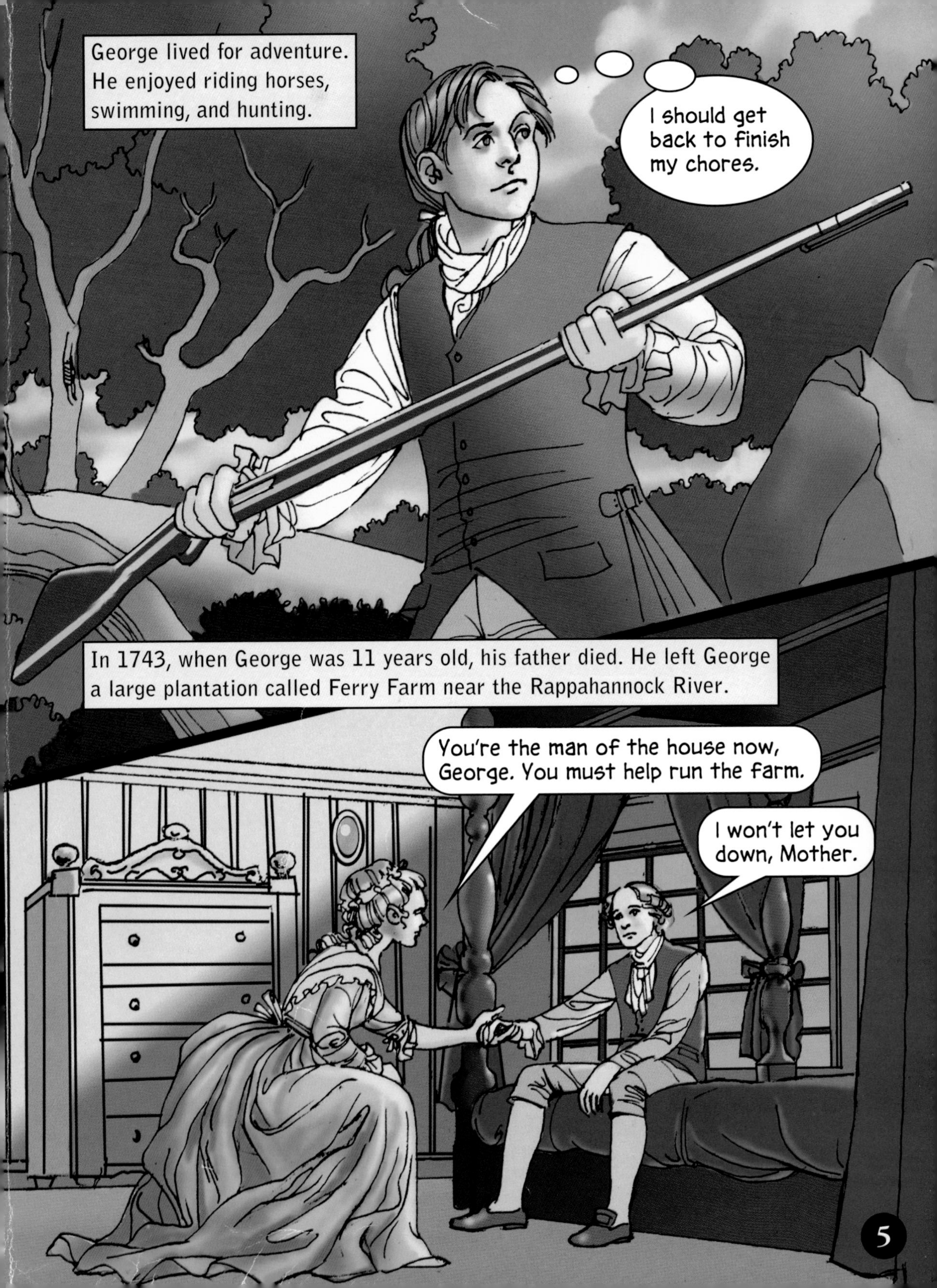
George lived for adventure. He enjoyed riding horses, swimming, and hunting.
I should get back to finish my chores.
In 1743, when George was 11 years old, his father died. He left George a large plantation called Ferry Farm near the Rappahannock River.
You're the man of the house now, George. You must help run the farm.
I won't let you down, Mother.

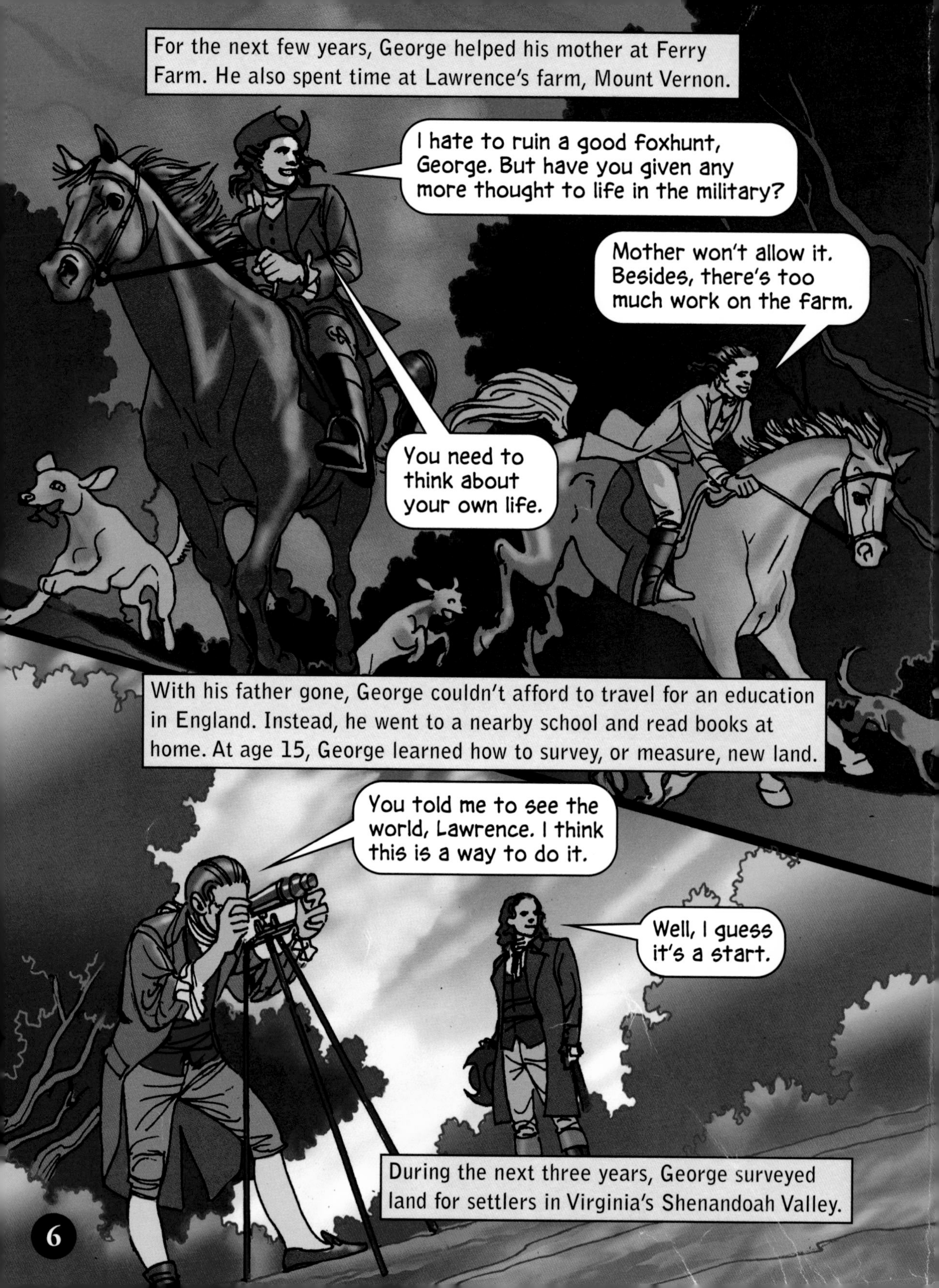
For the next few years, George helped his mother at Ferry Farm. He also spent time at Lawrence's farm, Mount Vernon.
I hate to ruin a good foxhunt, George. But have you given any more thought to life in the military?
Mother won't allow it. Besides, there's too much work on the farm.
You need to think about your own life.
With his father gone, George couldn't afford to travel for an education in England. Instead, he went to a nearby school and read books at home. At age 15, George learned how to survey, or measure, new land.
You told me to see the world, Lawrence. I think this is a way to do it.
Well, I guess it's a start.
During the next three years, George surveyed land for settlers in Virginia's Shenandoah Valley.

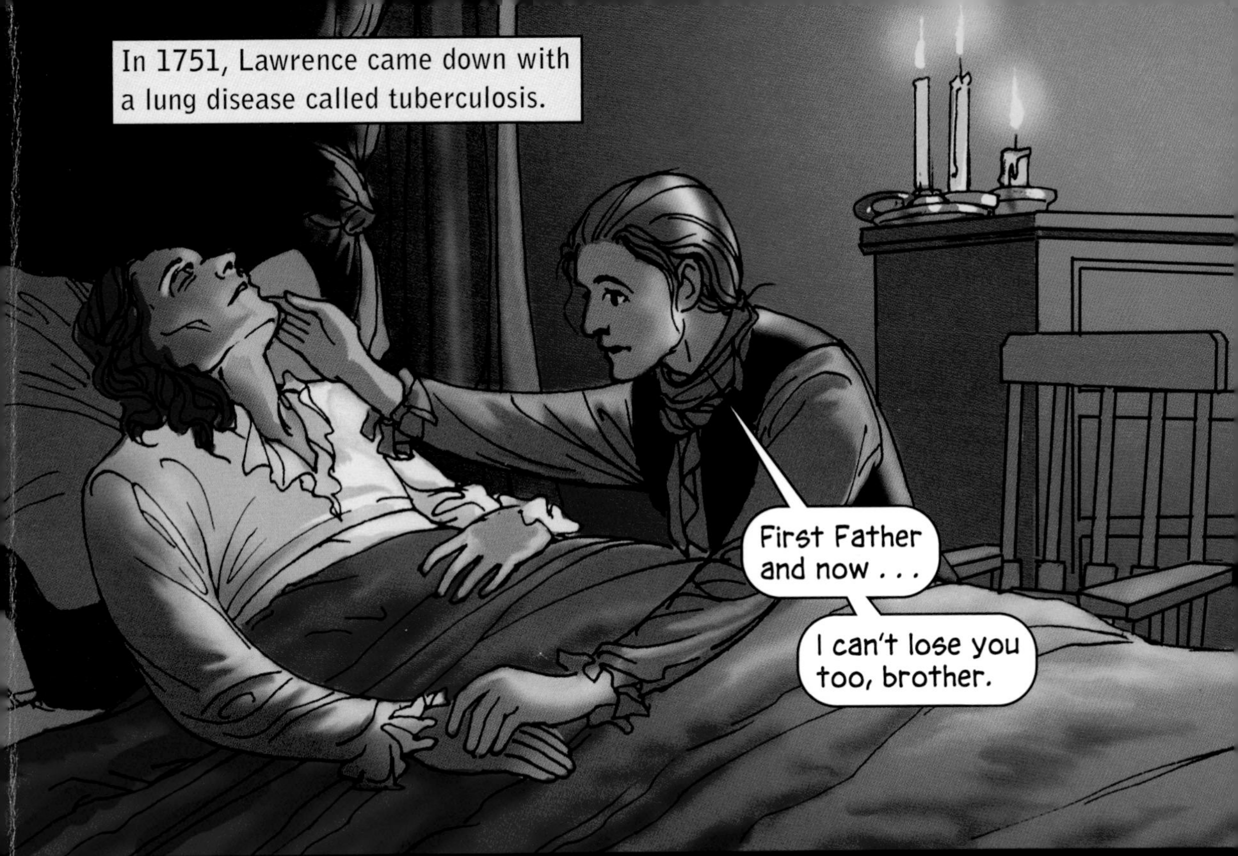
In 1751, Lawrence came down with a lung disease called tuberculosis.
First Father and now . . .
I can't lose you too, brother.

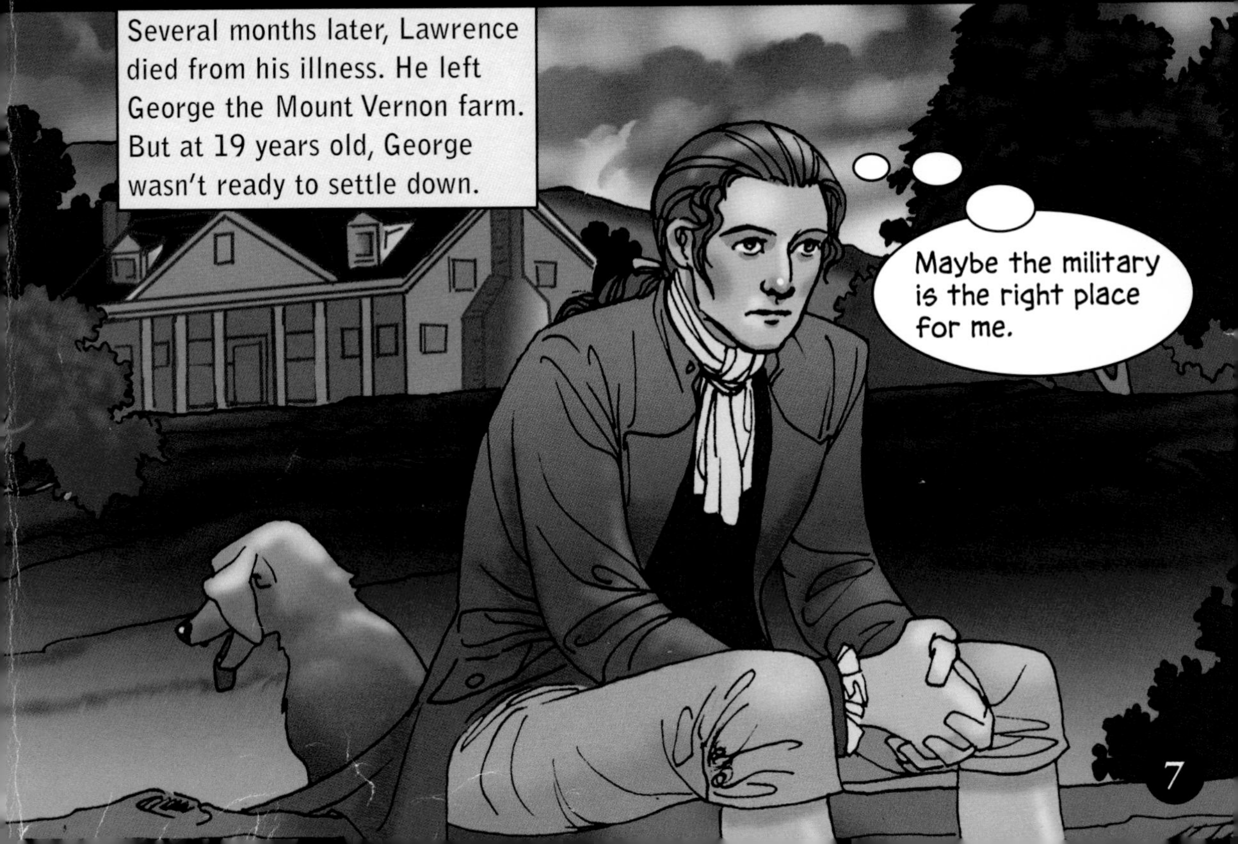
Several months later, Lawrence died from his illness. He left George the Mount Vernon farm. But at 19 years old, George wasn't ready to settle down.
Maybe the military is the right place for me.

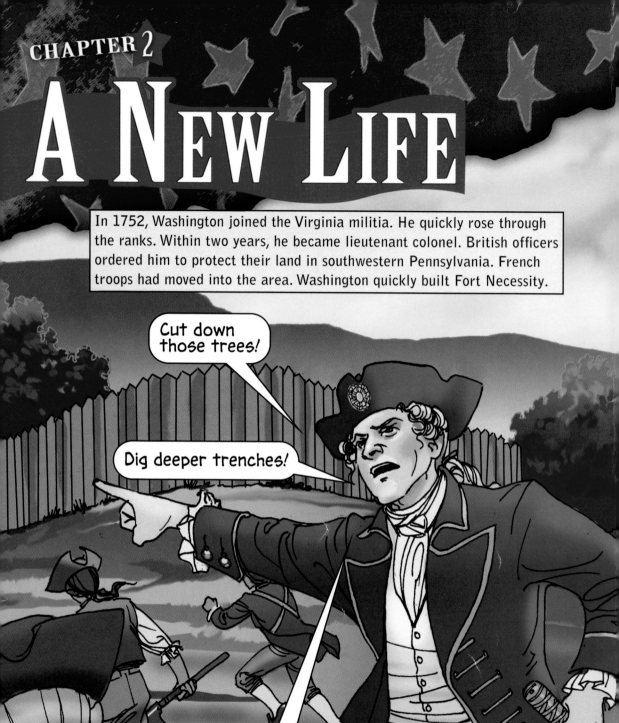

CHAPTER 2
A NEW LIFE

In 1752, Washington joined the Virginia militia. He quickly rose through the ranks. Within two years, he became lieutenant colonel. British officers ordered him to protect their land in southwestern Pennsylvania. French troops had moved into the area. Washington quickly built Fort Necessity.

Cut down those trees!

Dig deeper trenches!

The French will attack soon!

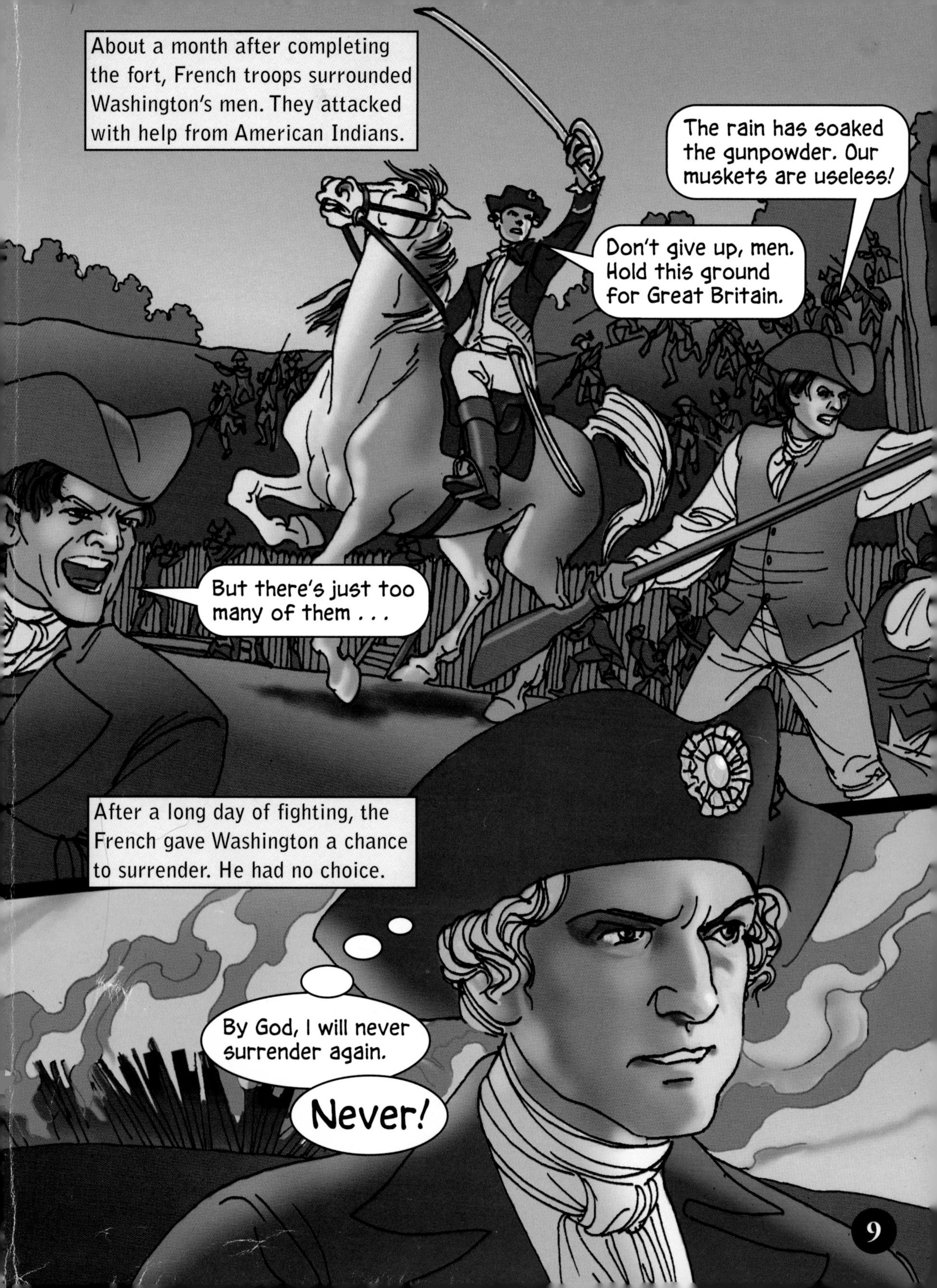

About a month after completing the fort, French troops surrounded Washington's men. They attacked with help from American Indians.
The rain has soaked the gunpowder. Our muskets are useless!
Don't give up, men. Hold this ground for Great Britain.
But there's just too many of them . . .
After a long day of fighting, the French gave Washington a chance to surrender. He had no choice.
By God, I will never surrender again.
Never!

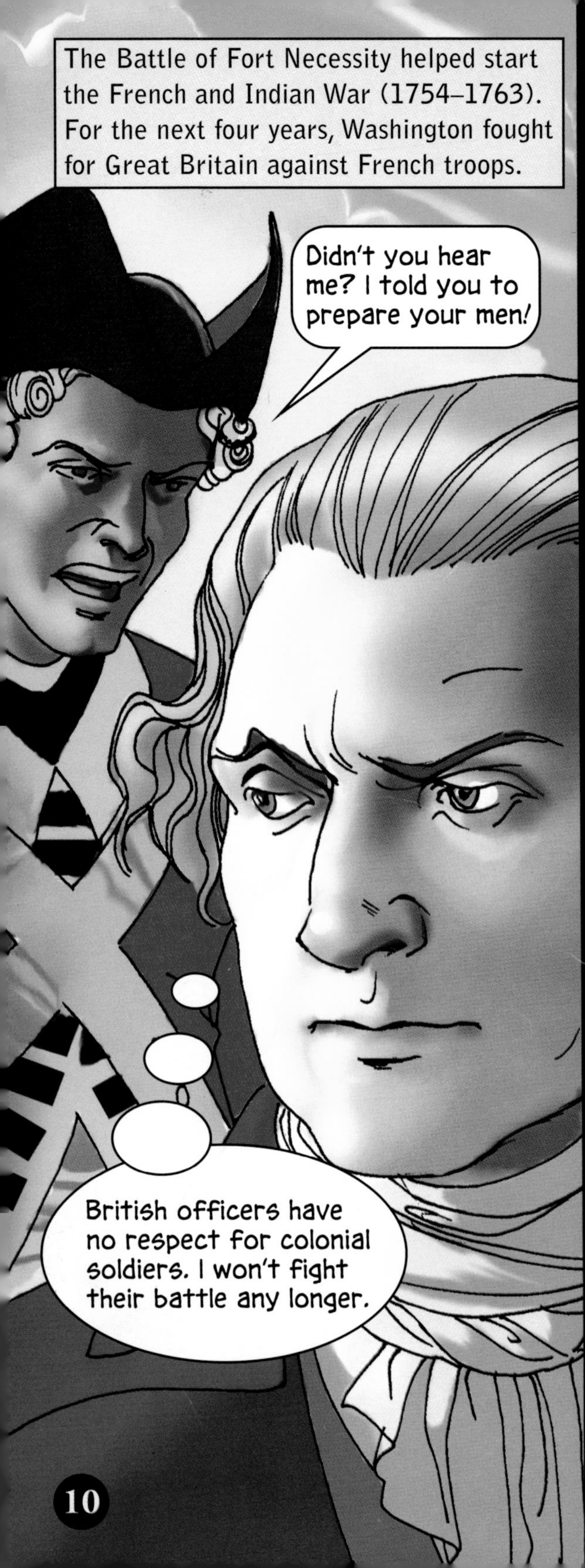
The Battle of Fort Necessity helped start the French and Indian War (1754–1763). For the next four years, Washington fought for Great Britain against French troops.
Didn't you hear me? I told you to prepare your men!
British officers have no respect for colonial soldiers. I won't fight their battle any longer.

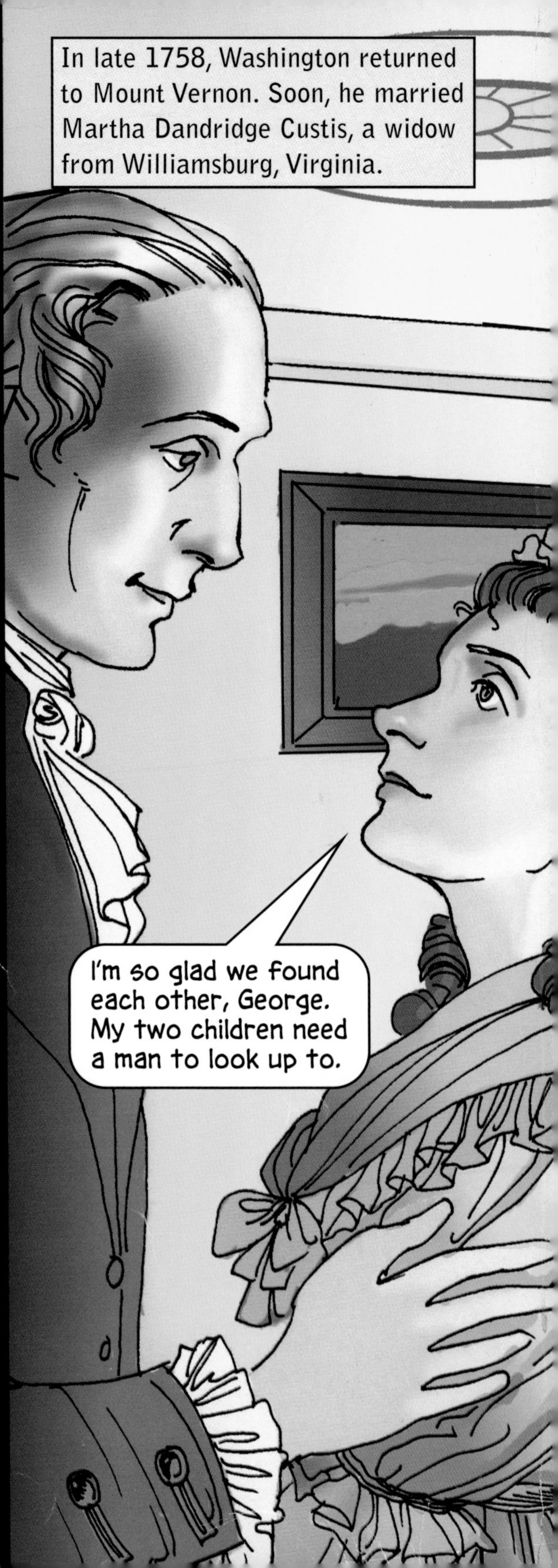
In late 1758, Washington returned to Mount Vernon. Soon, he married Martha Dandridge Custis, a widow from Williamsburg, Virginia.
I'm so glad we found each other, George. My two children need a man to look up to.

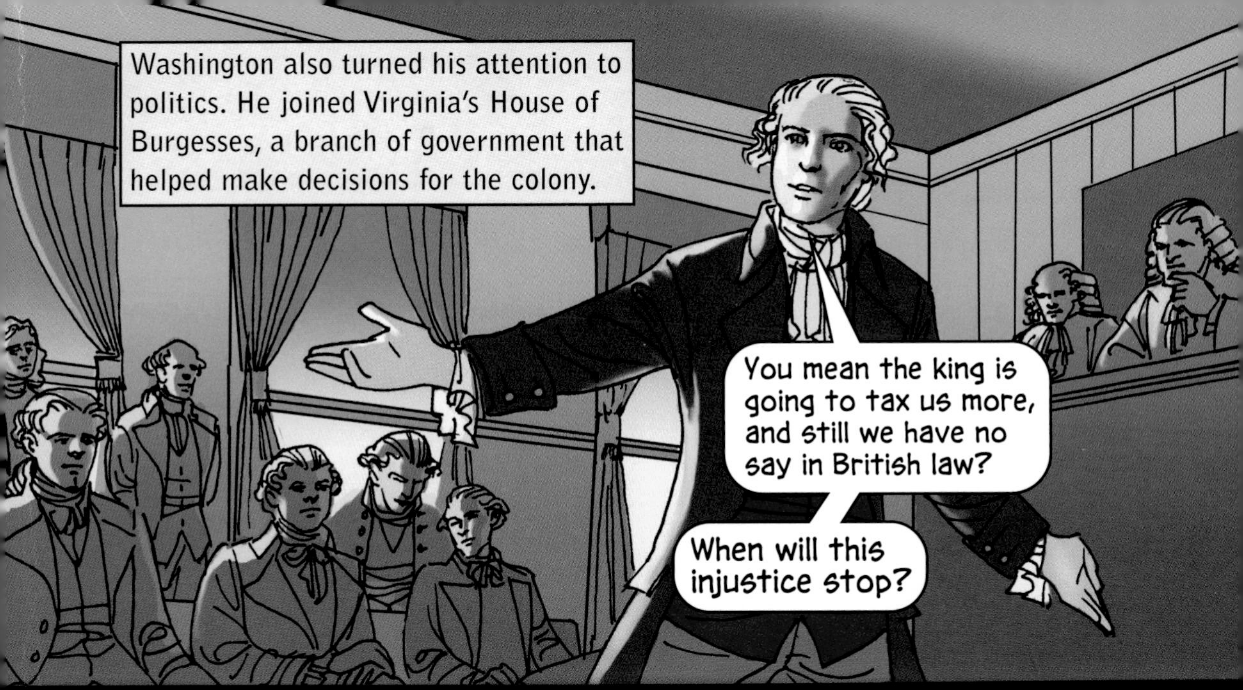
Washington also turned his attention to politics. He joined Virginia's House of Burgesses, a branch of government that helped make decisions for the colony.
You mean the king is going to tax us more, and still we have no say in British law?
When will this injustice stop?

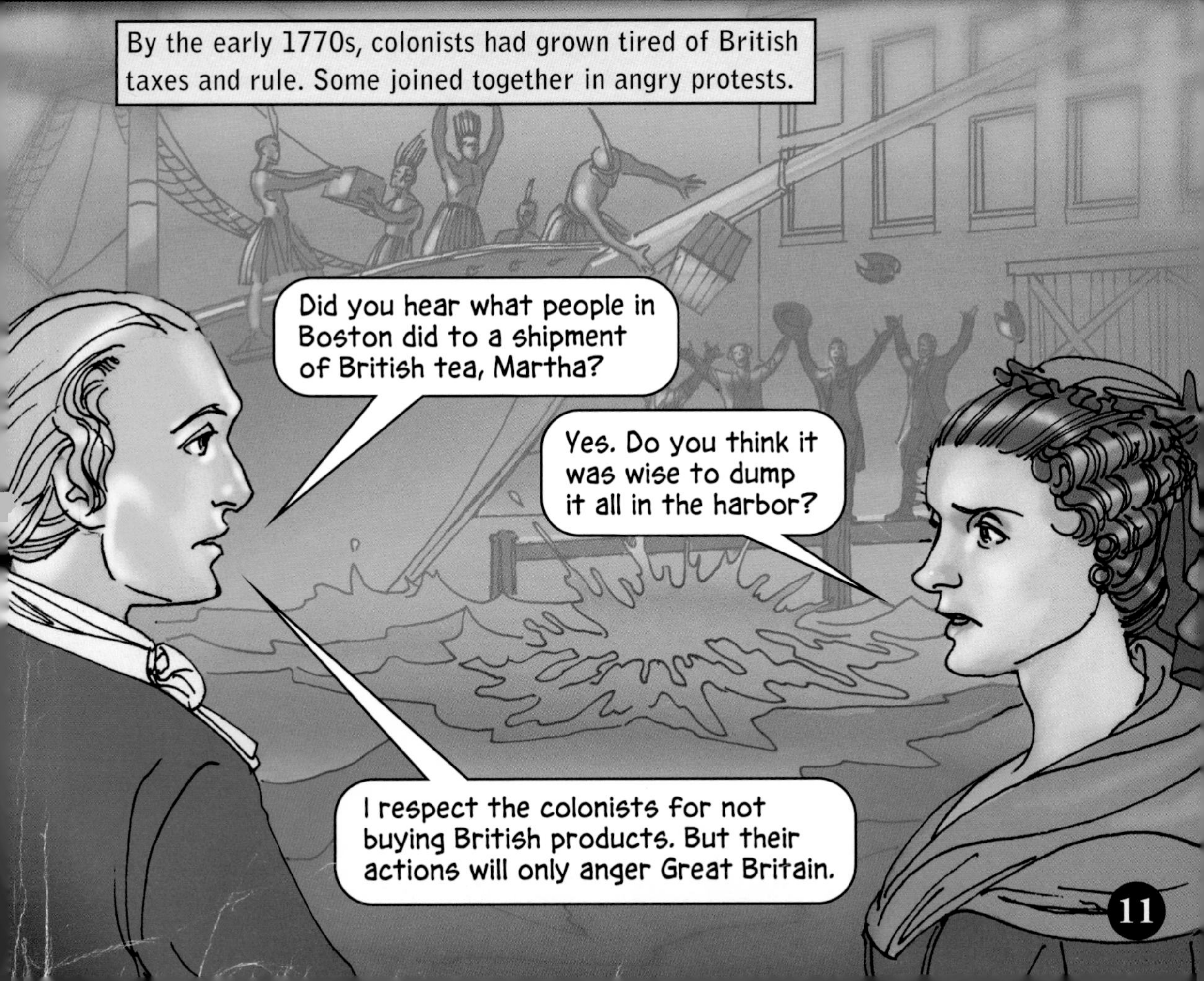
By the early 1770s, colonists had grown tired of British taxes and rule. Some joined together in angry protests.
Did you hear what people in Boston did to a shipment of British tea, Martha?
Yes. Do you think it was wise to dump it all in the harbor?
I respect the colonists for not buying British products. But their actions will only anger Great Britain.

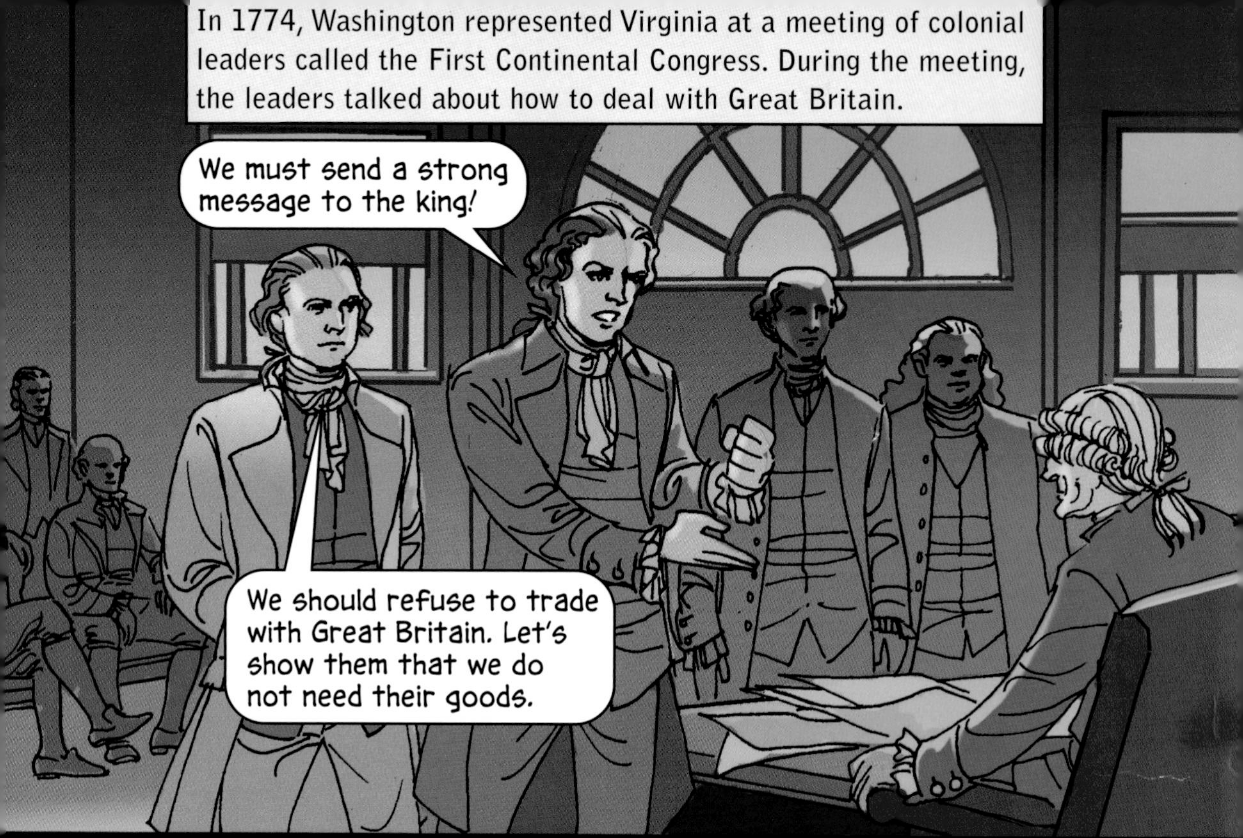
In 1774, Washington represented Virginia at a meeting of colonial leaders called the First Continental Congress. During the meeting, the leaders talked about how to deal with Great Britain.
We must send a strong message to the king!
We should refuse to trade with Great Britain. Let's show them that we do not need their goods.

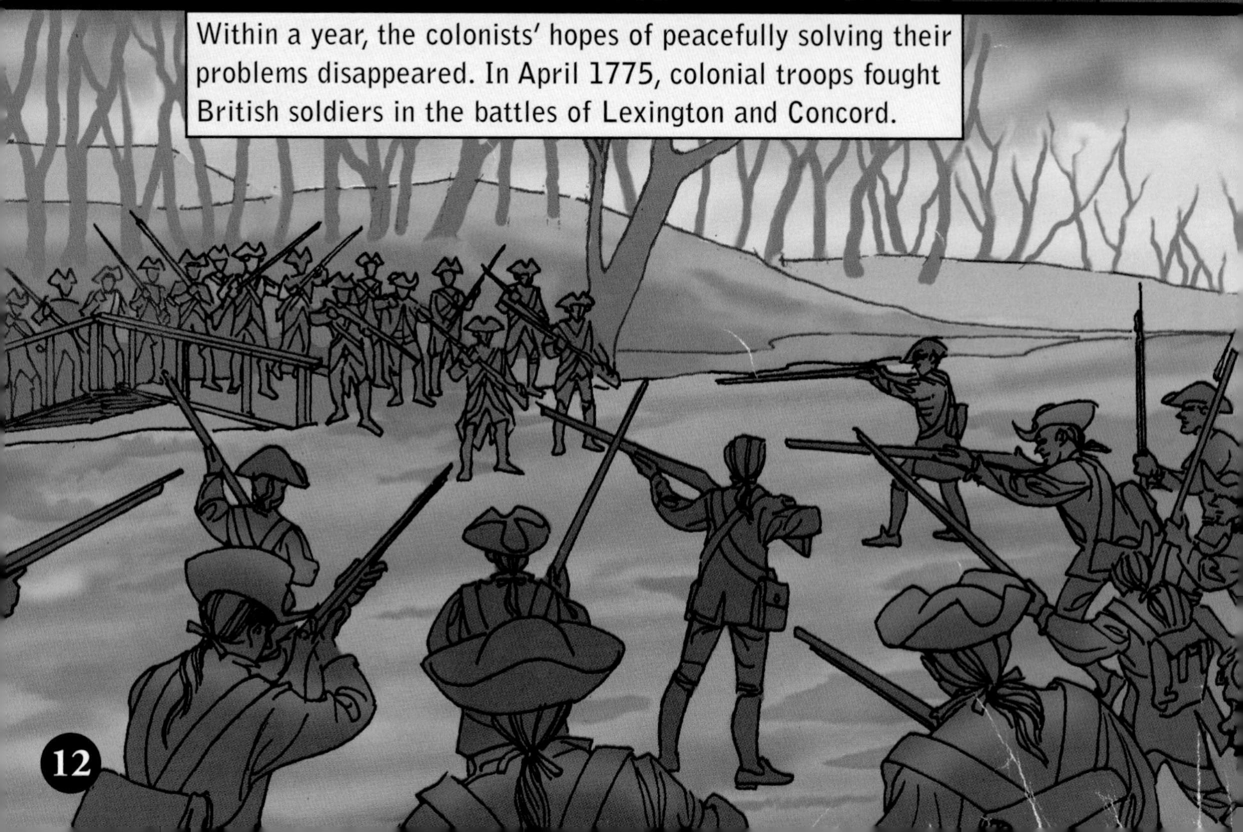
Within a year, the colonists' hopes of peacefully solving their problems disappeared. In April 1775, colonial troops fought British soldiers in the battles of Lexington and Concord.

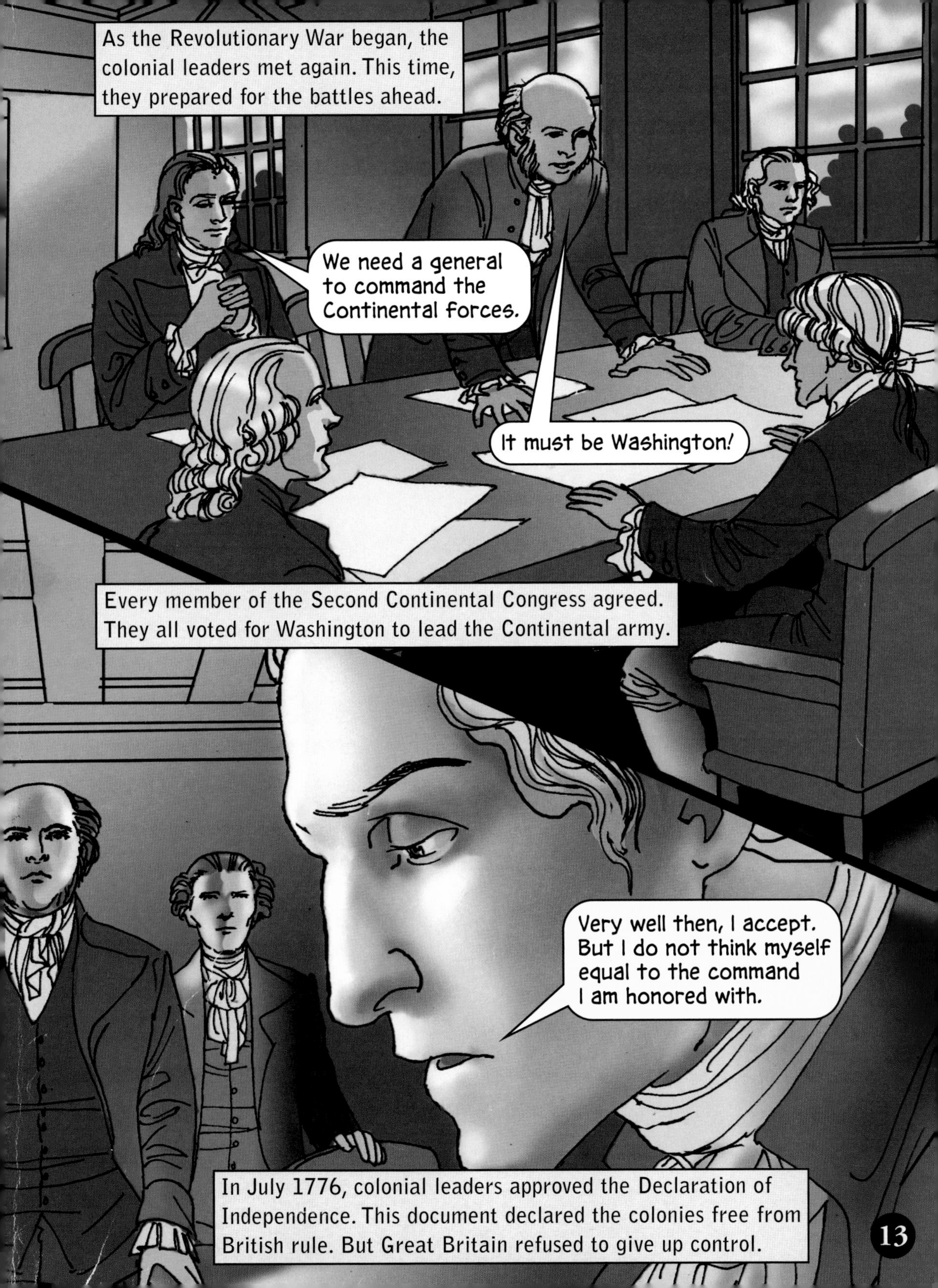
As the Revolutionary War began, the colonial leaders met again. This time, they prepared for the battles ahead.
We need a general to command the Continental forces.
It must be Washington!
Every member of the Second Continental Congress agreed. They all voted for Washington to lead the Continental army.
Very well then, I accept. But I do not think myself equal to the command I am honored with.
In July 1776, colonial leaders approved the Declaration of Independence. This document declared the colonies free from British rule. But Great Britain refused to give up control.

CHAPTER 3
GENERAL WASHINGTON

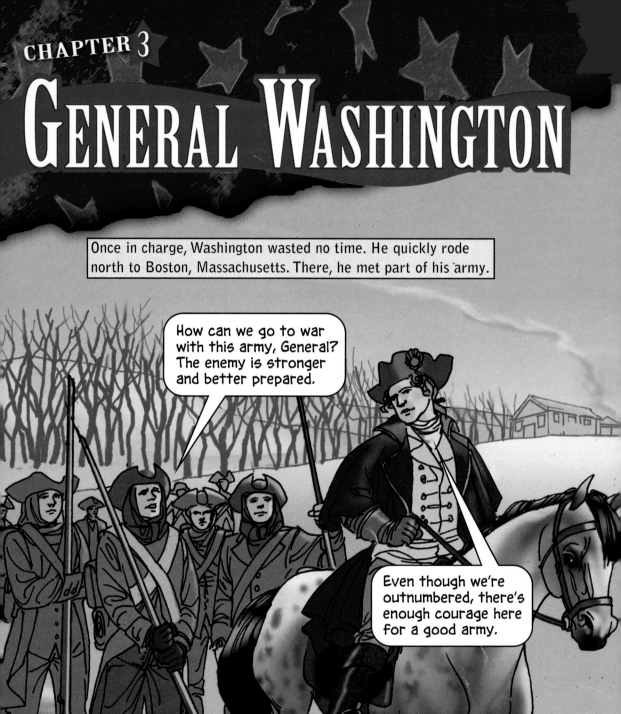

Once in charge, Washington wasted no time. He quickly rode north to Boston, Massachusetts. There, he met part of his army.

How can we go to war with this army, General? The enemy is stronger and better prepared.

Even though we're outnumbered, there's enough courage here for a good army.

But early on, the war didn't go well for the colonists. By November 1776, they had retreated to Trenton, New Jersey.

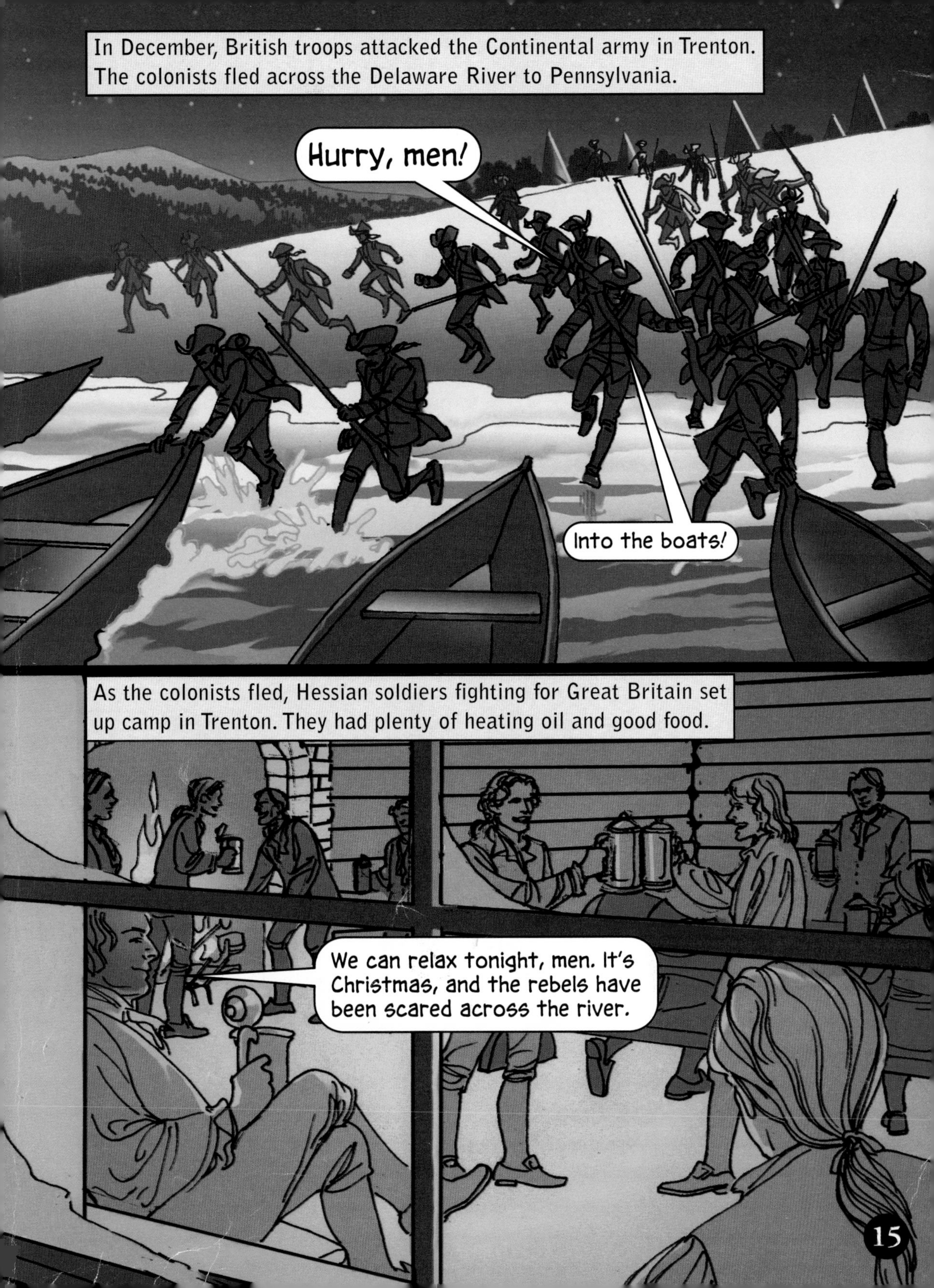
In December, British troops attacked the Continental army in Trenton. The colonists fled across the Delaware River to Pennsylvania.
Hurry, men!
Into the boats!
As the colonists fled, Hessian soldiers fighting for Great Britain set up camp in Trenton. They had plenty of heating oil and good food.
We can relax tonight, men. It's Christmas, and the rebels have been scared across the river.

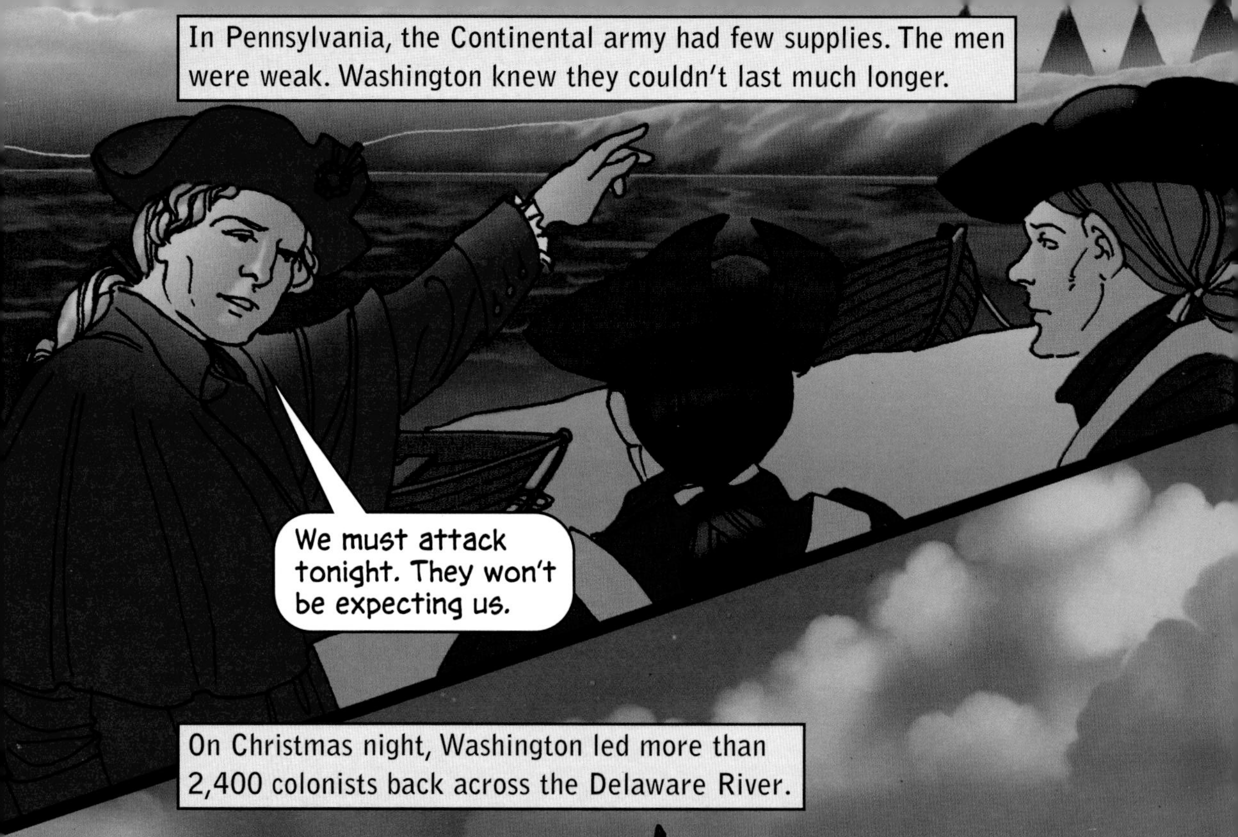
In Pennsylvania, the Continental army had few supplies. The men were weak. Washington knew they couldn't last much longer.
We must attack tonight. They won't be expecting us.

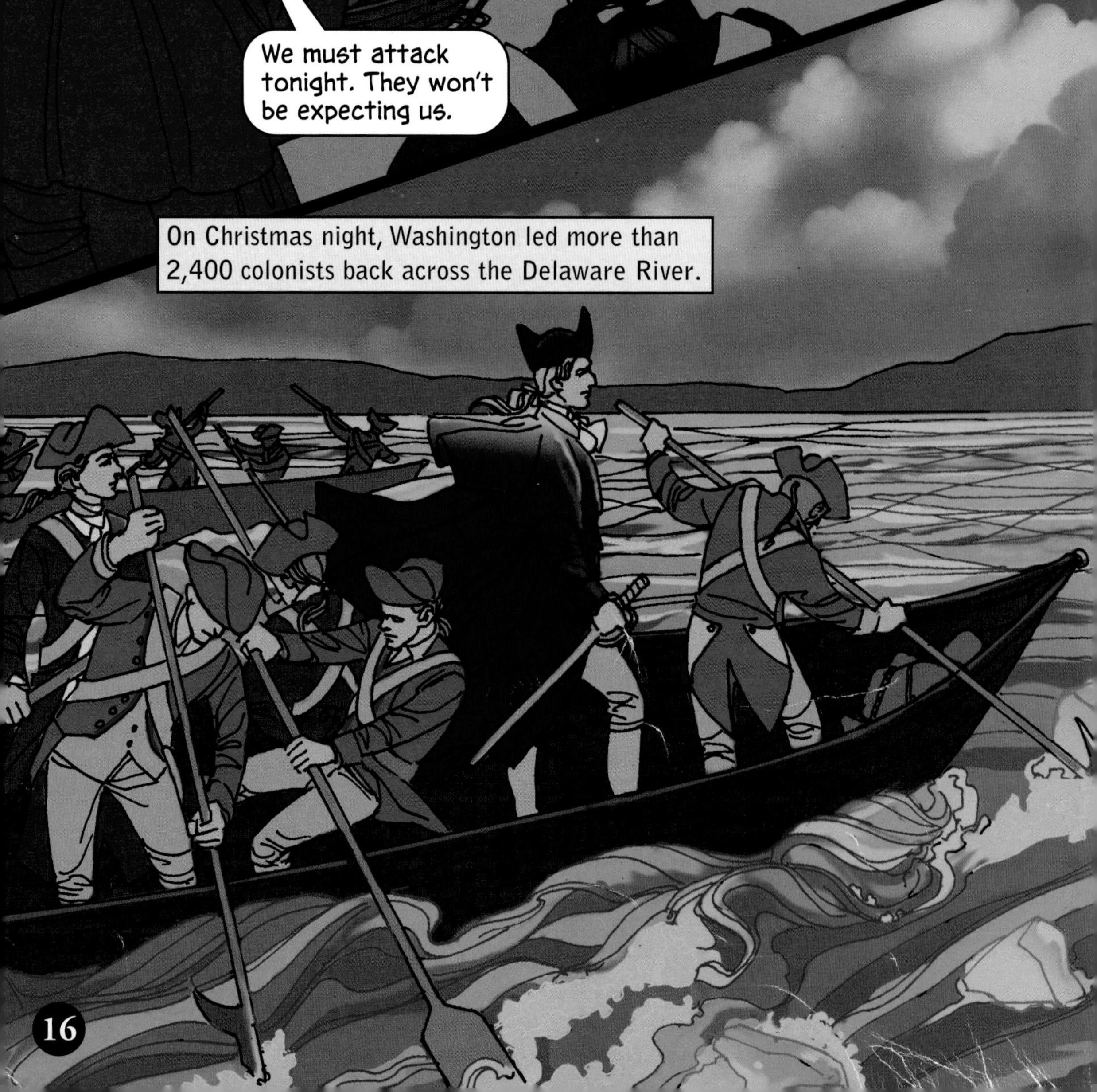
On Christmas night, Washington led more than 2,400 colonists back across the Delaware River.

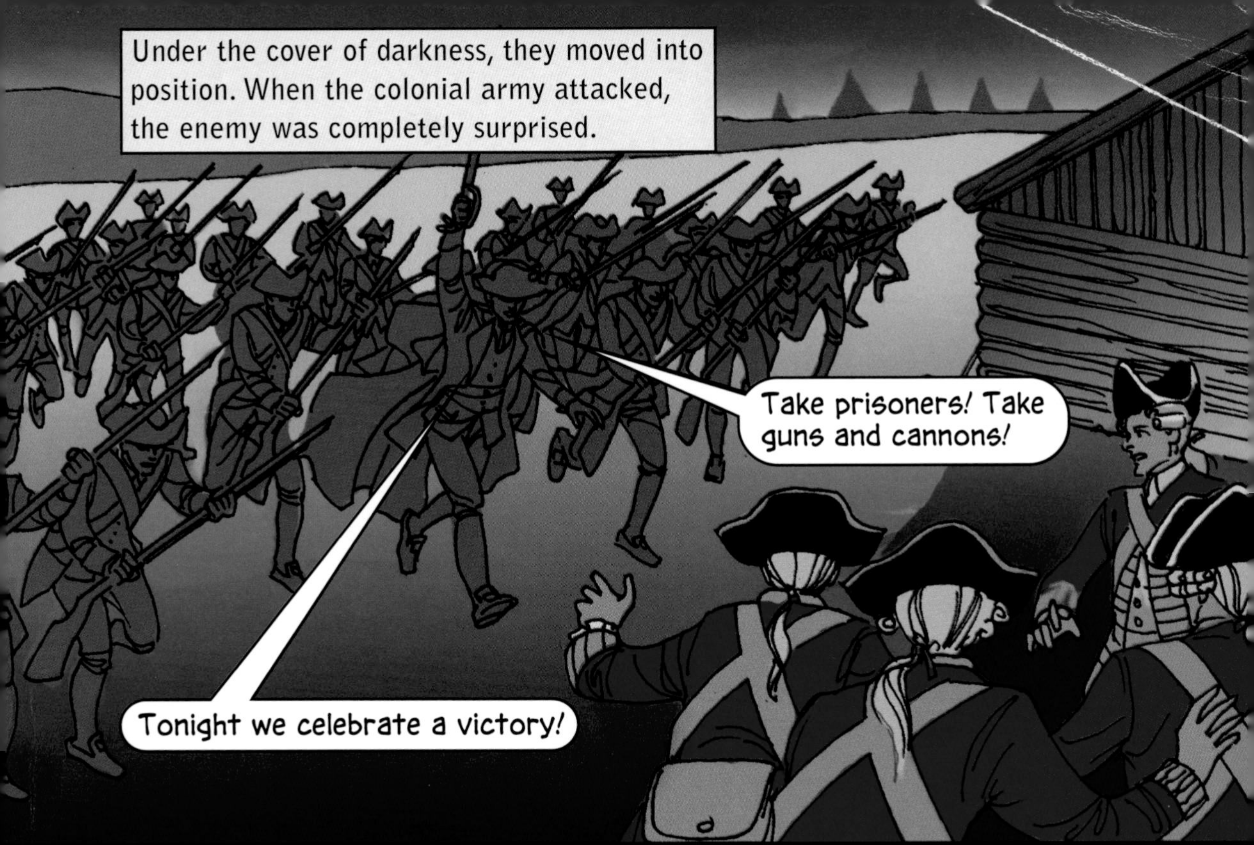
Under the cover of darkness, they moved into position. When the colonial army attacked, the enemy was completely surprised.
Tonight we celebrate a victory!
Take prisoners! Take guns and cannons!

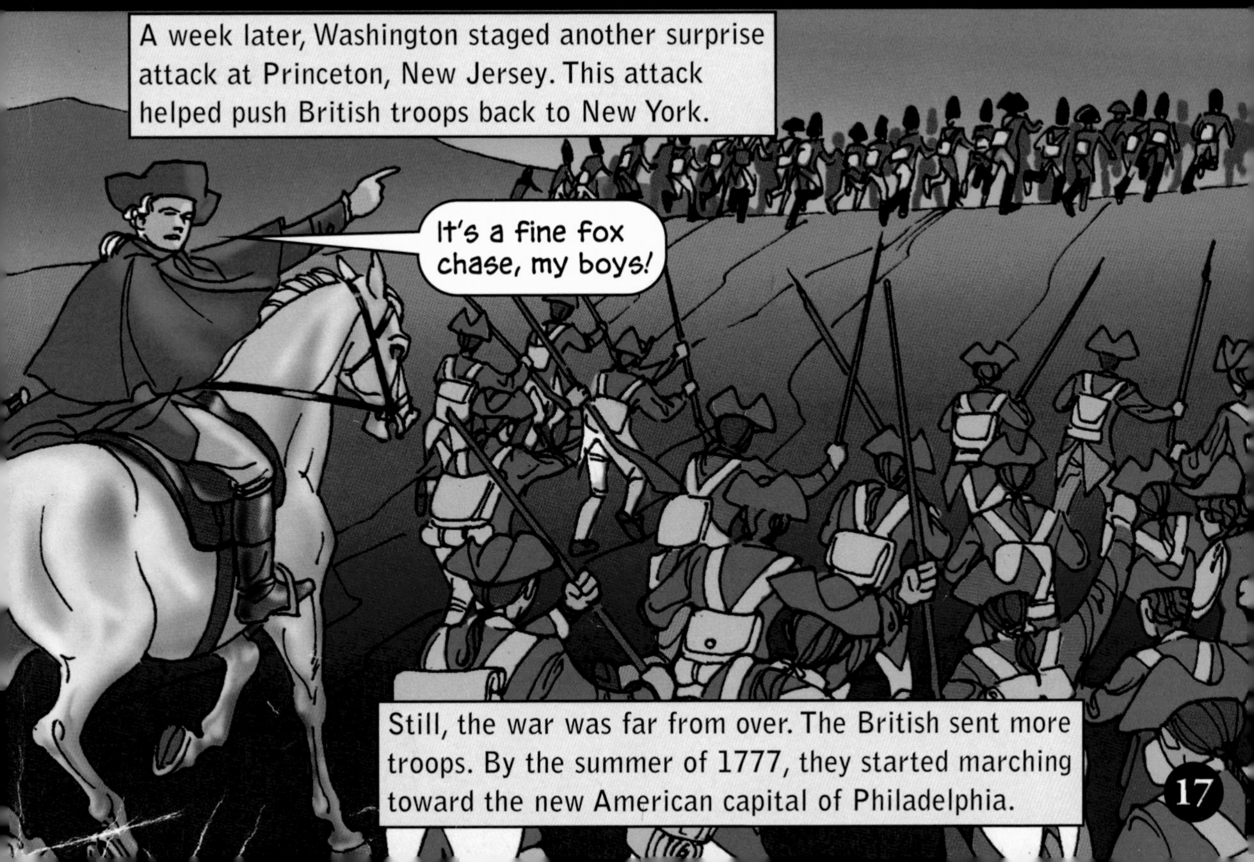
A week later, Washington staged another surprise attack at Princeton, New Jersey. This attack helped push British troops back to New York.
It's a fine fox chase, my boys!
Still, the war was far from over. The British sent more troops. By the summer of 1777, they started marching toward the new American capital of Philadelphia.

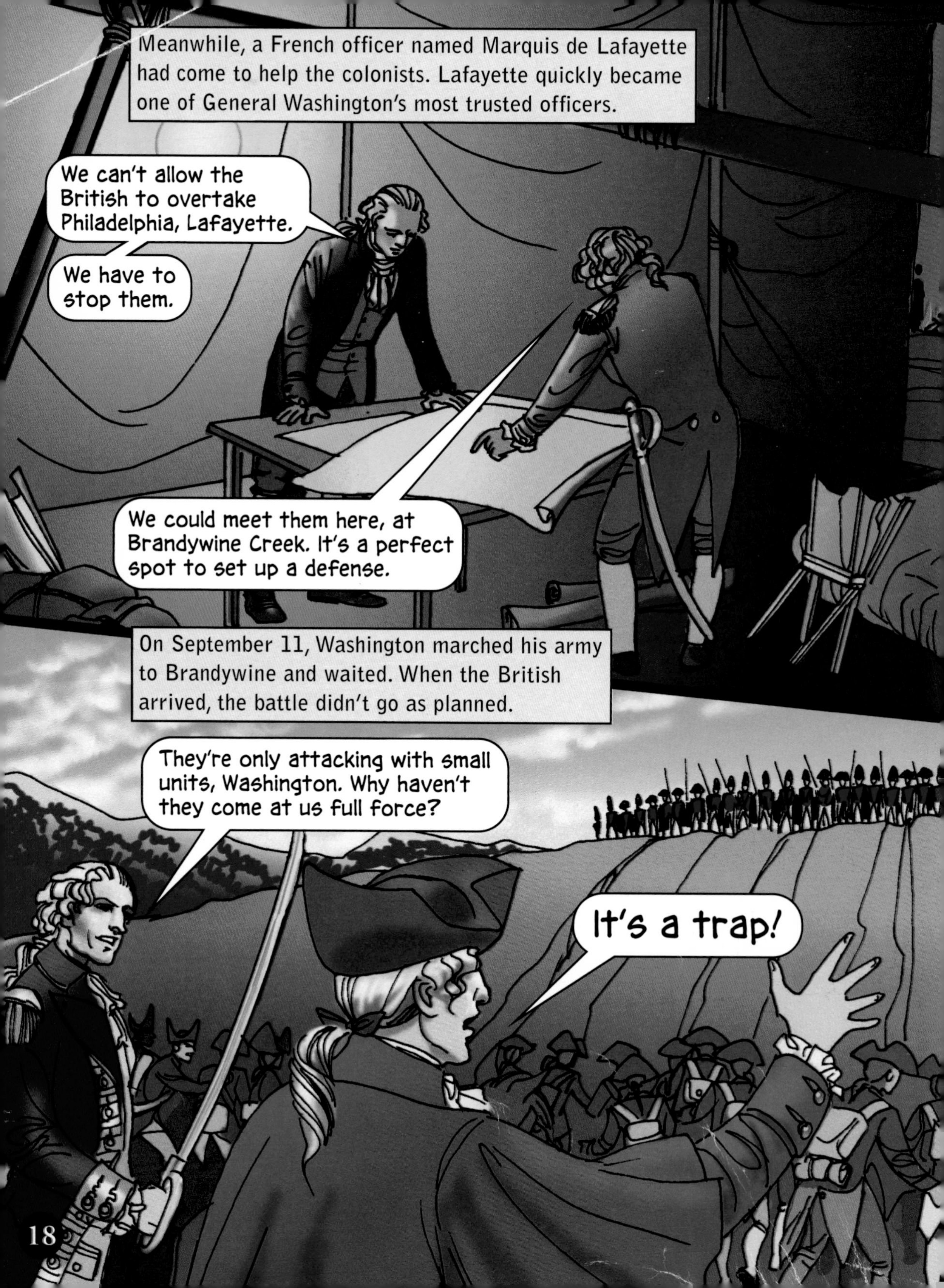
Meanwhile, a French officer named Marquis de Lafayette had come to help the colonists. Lafayette quickly became one of General Washington's most trusted officers.
We can't allow the British to overtake Philadelphia, Lafayette.
We have to stop them.
We could meet them here, at Brandywine Creek. It's a perfect spot to set up a defense.
On September 11, Washington marched his army to Brandywine and waited. When the British arrived, the battle didn't go as planned.
They're only attacking with small units, Washington. Why haven't they come at us full force?
It's a trap!

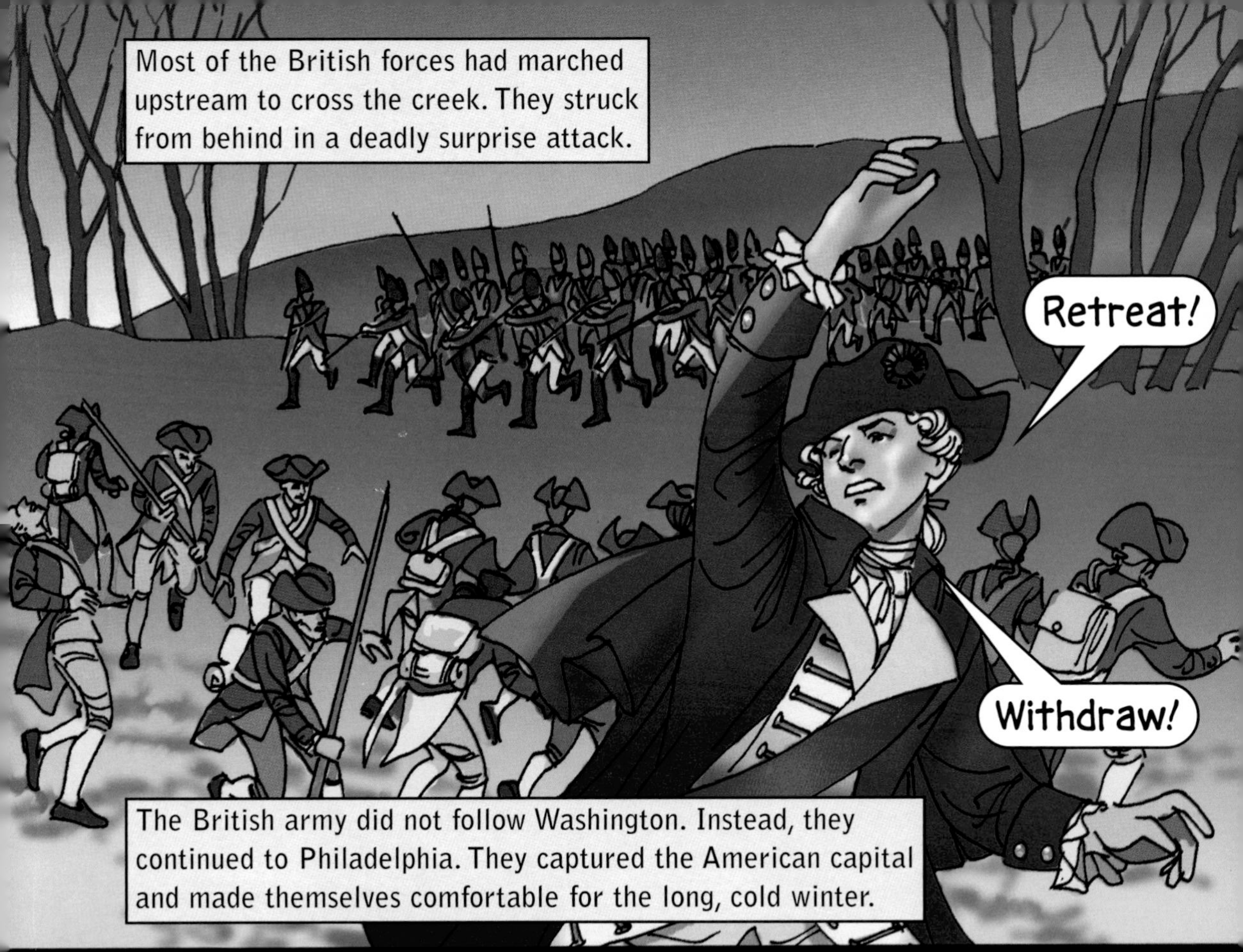
Most of the British forces had marched upstream to cross the creek. They struck from behind in a deadly surprise attack.
Retreat!
Withdraw!
The British army did not follow Washington. Instead, they continued to Philadelphia. They captured the American capital and made themselves comfortable for the long, cold winter.

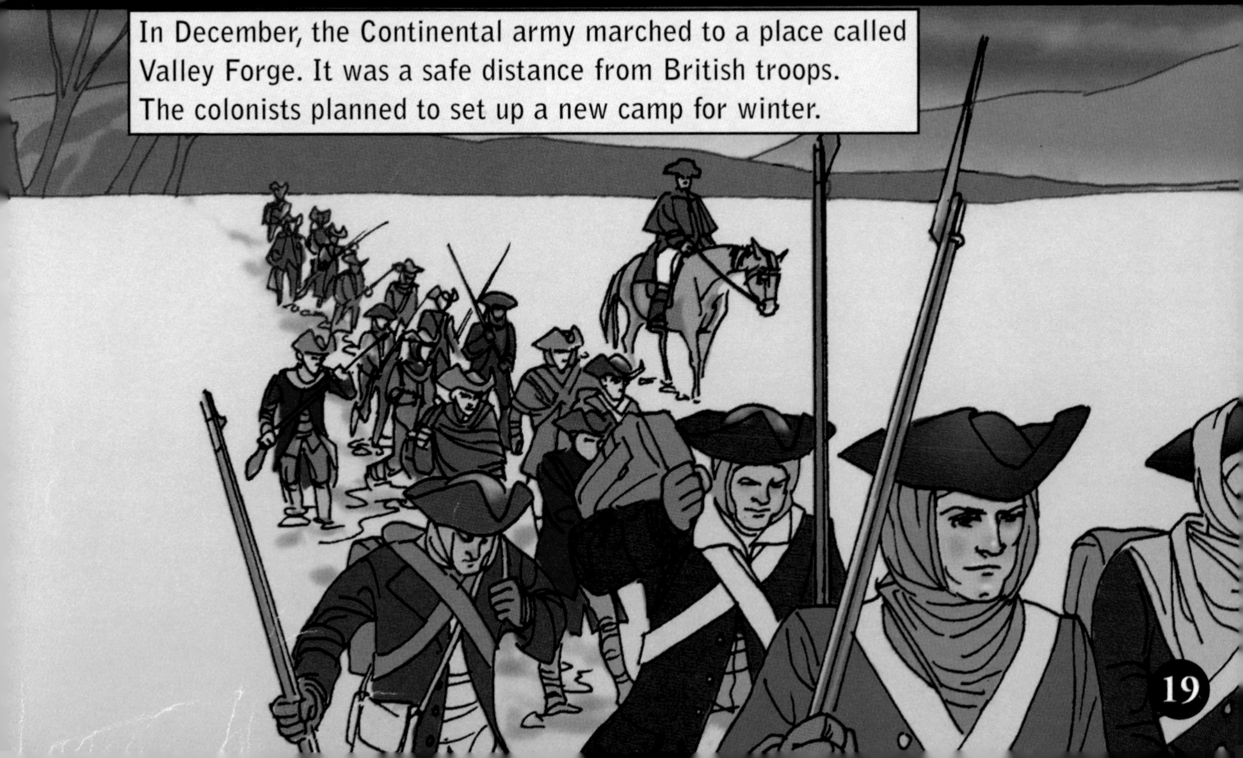
In December, the Continental army marched to a place called Valley Forge. It was a safe distance from British troops. The colonists planned to set up a new camp for winter.

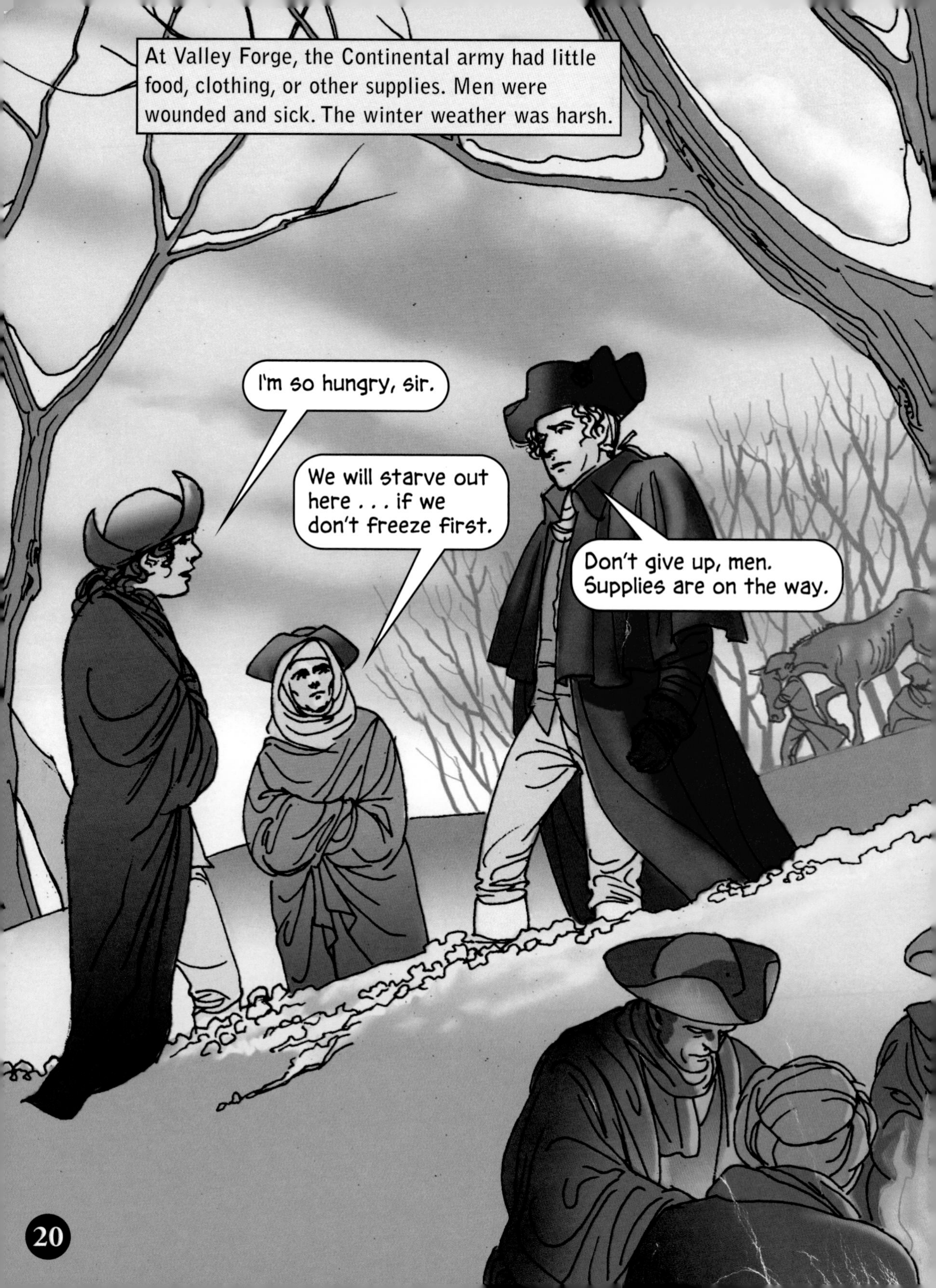
At Valley Forge, the Continental army had little food, clothing, or other supplies. Men were wounded and sick. The winter weather was harsh.
I'm so hungry, sir.
We will starve out here . . . if we don't freeze first.
Don't give up, men. Supplies are on the way.

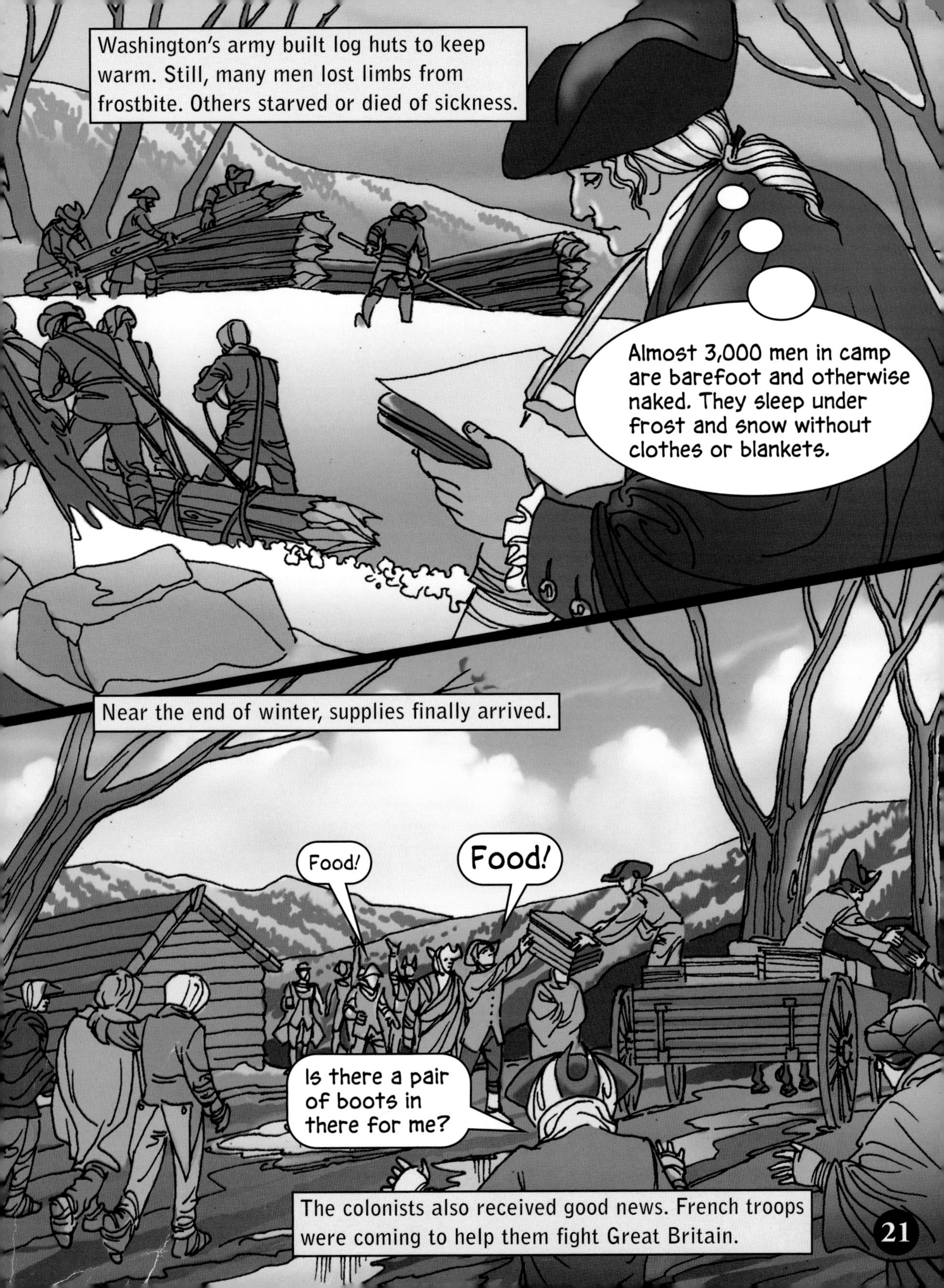

Washington's army built log huts to keep warm. Still, many men lost limbs from frostbite. Others starved or died of sickness.
Almost 3,000 men in camp are barefoot and otherwise naked. They sleep under frost and snow without clothes or blankets.
Near the end of winter, supplies finally arrived.
Food!
Food!
Is there a pair of boots in there for me?
The colonists also received good news. French troops were coming to help them fight Great Britain.

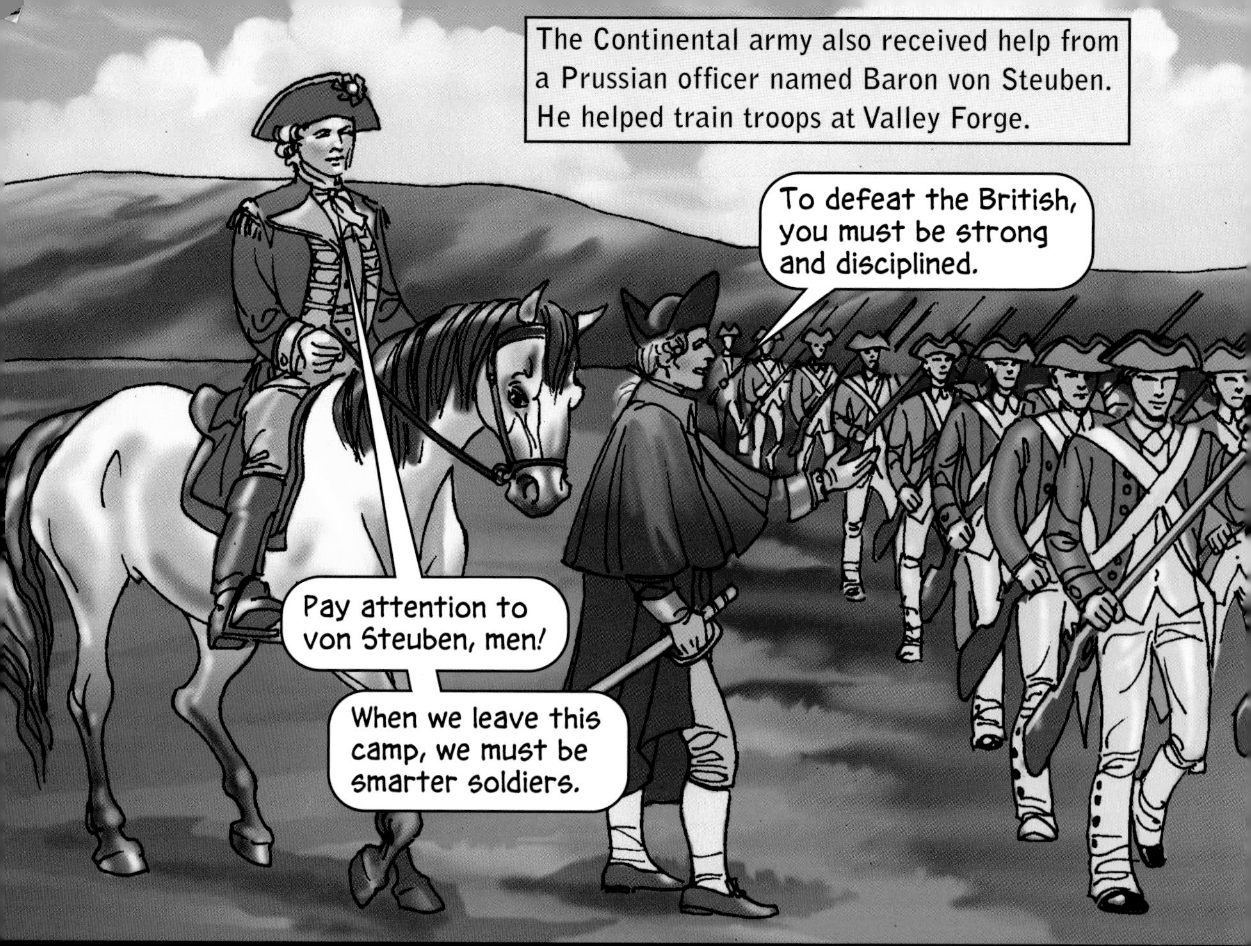
The Continental army also received help from a Prussian officer named Baron von Steuben. He helped train troops at Valley Forge.
To defeat the British, you must be strong and disciplined.
Pay attention to von Steuben, men!
When we leave this camp, we must be smarter soldiers.

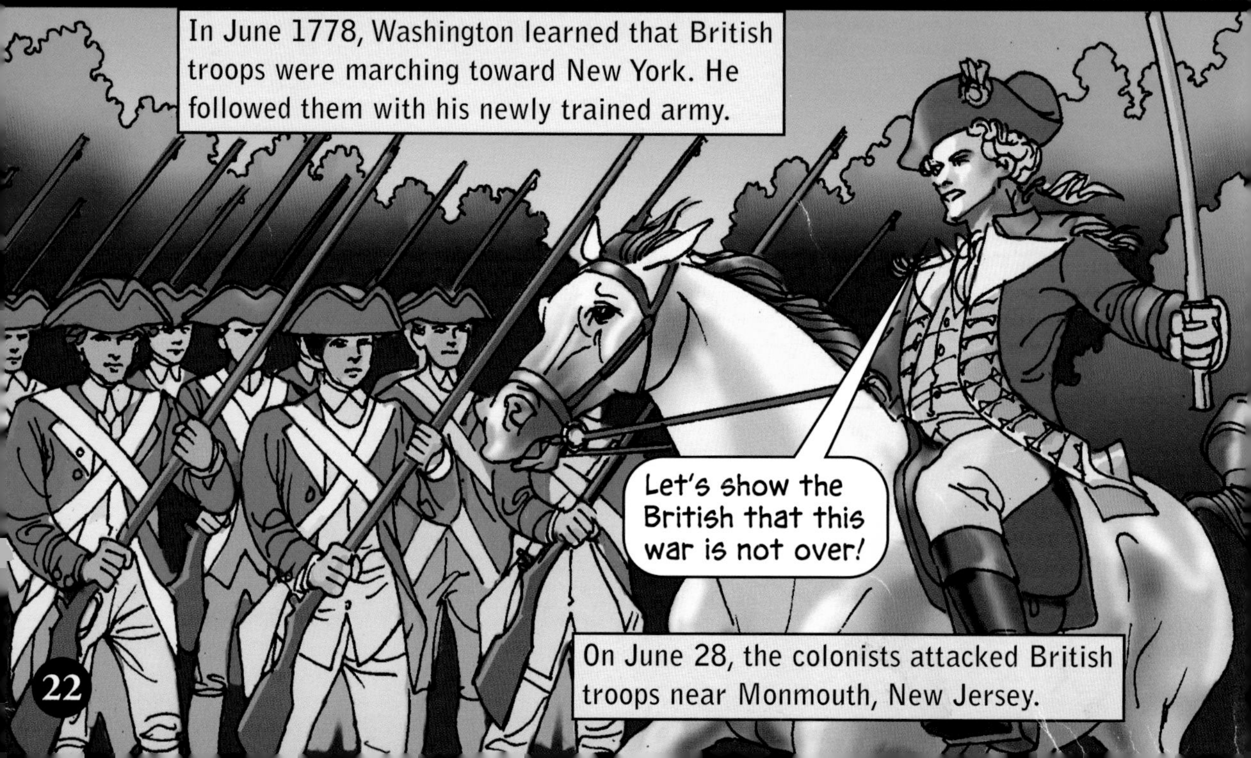
In June 1778, Washington learned that British troops were marching toward New York. He followed them with his newly trained army.
Let's show the British that this war is not over!
On June 28, the colonists attacked British troops near Monmouth, New Jersey.

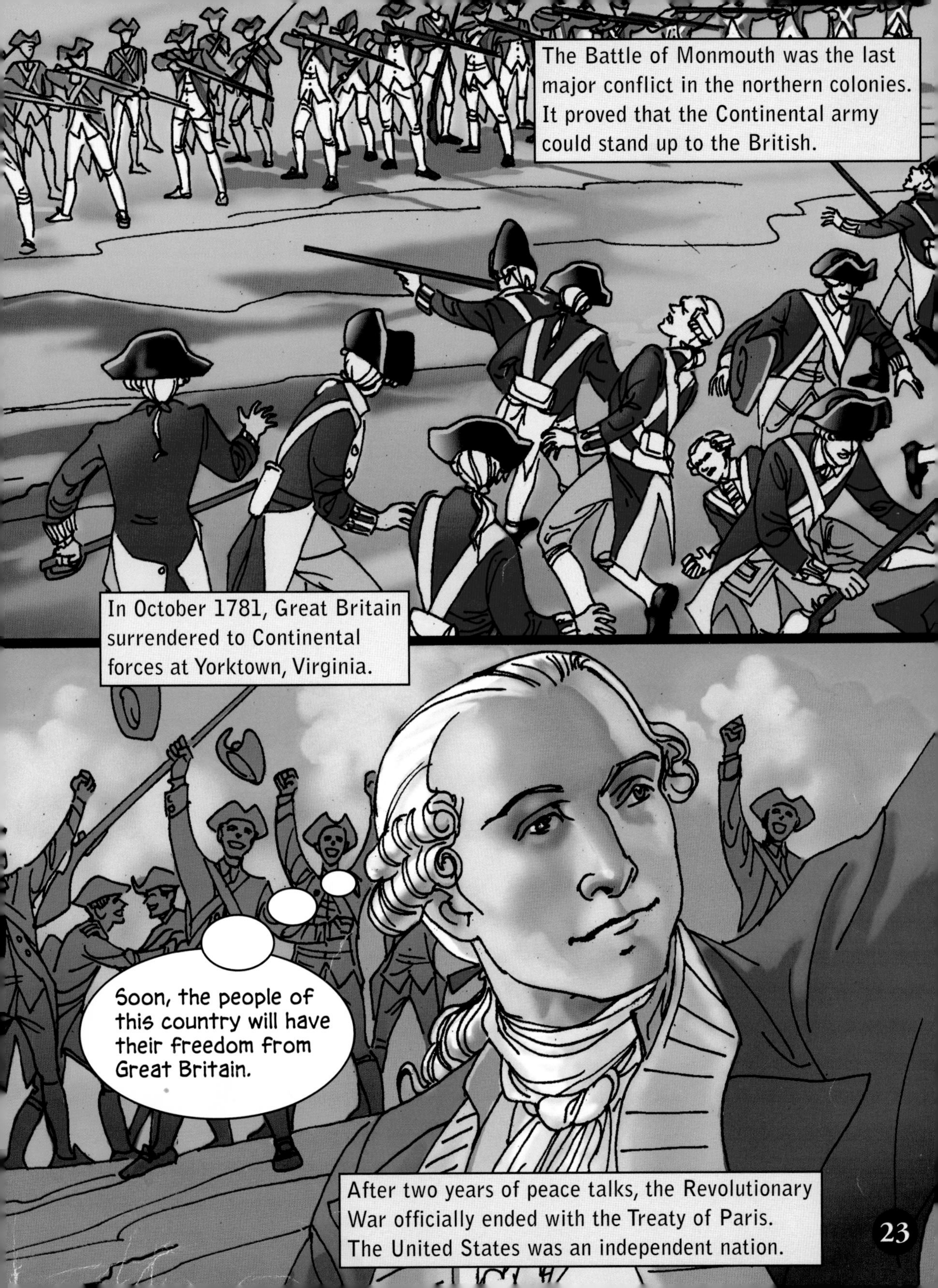
The Battle of Monmouth was the last major conflict in the northern colonies. It proved that the Continental army could stand up to the British.
In October 1781, Great Britain surrendered to Continental forces at Yorktown, Virginia.
Soon, the people of this country will have their freedom from Great Britain.
After two years of peace talks, the Revolutionary War officially ended with the Treaty of Paris. The United States was an independent nation.

CHAPTER 4
THE FIRST PRESIDENT

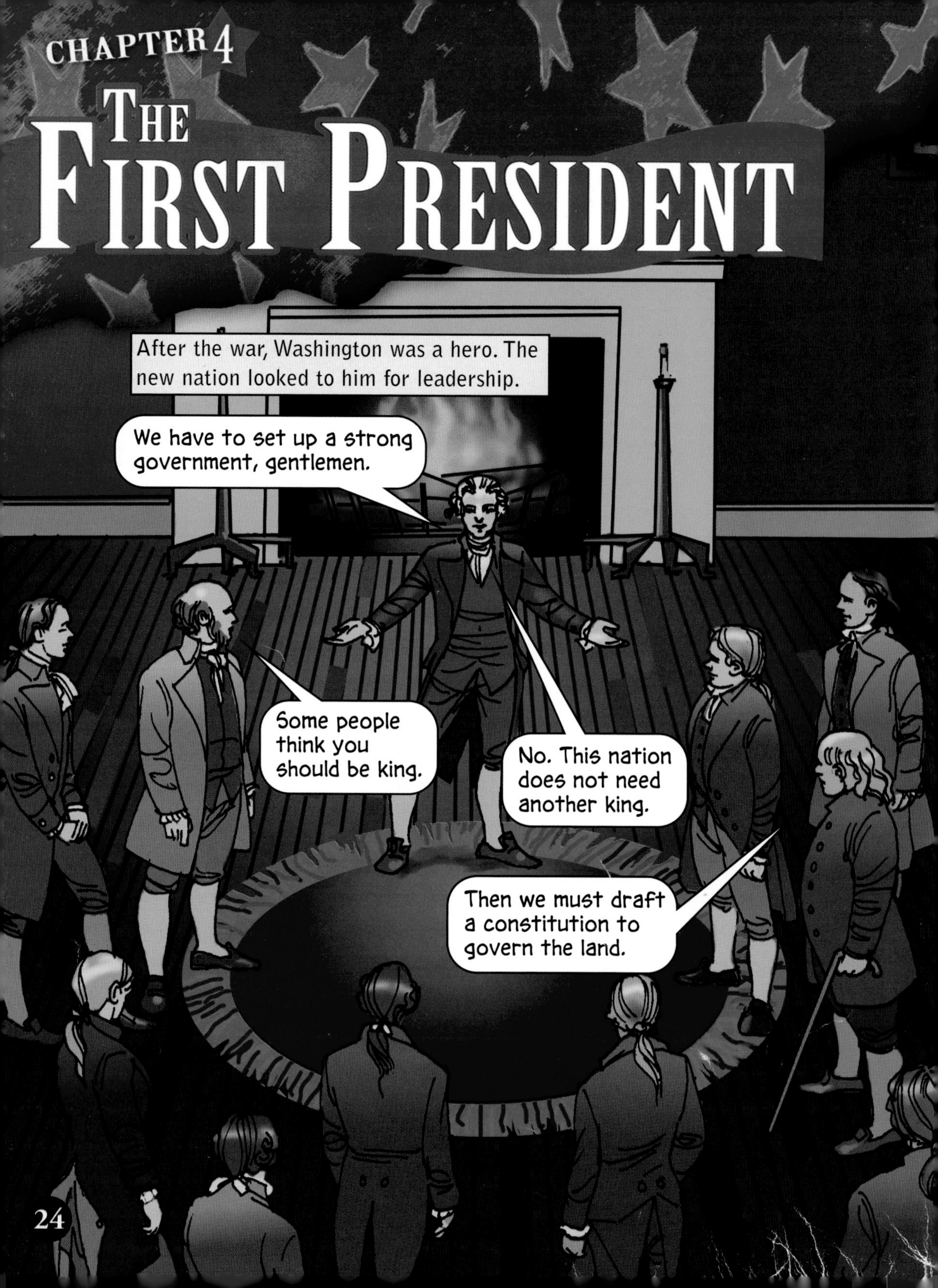
After the war, Washington was a hero. The new nation looked to him for leadership.
We have to set up a strong government, gentlemen.
Some people think you should be king.
No. This nation does not need another king.
Then we must draft a constitution to govern the land.

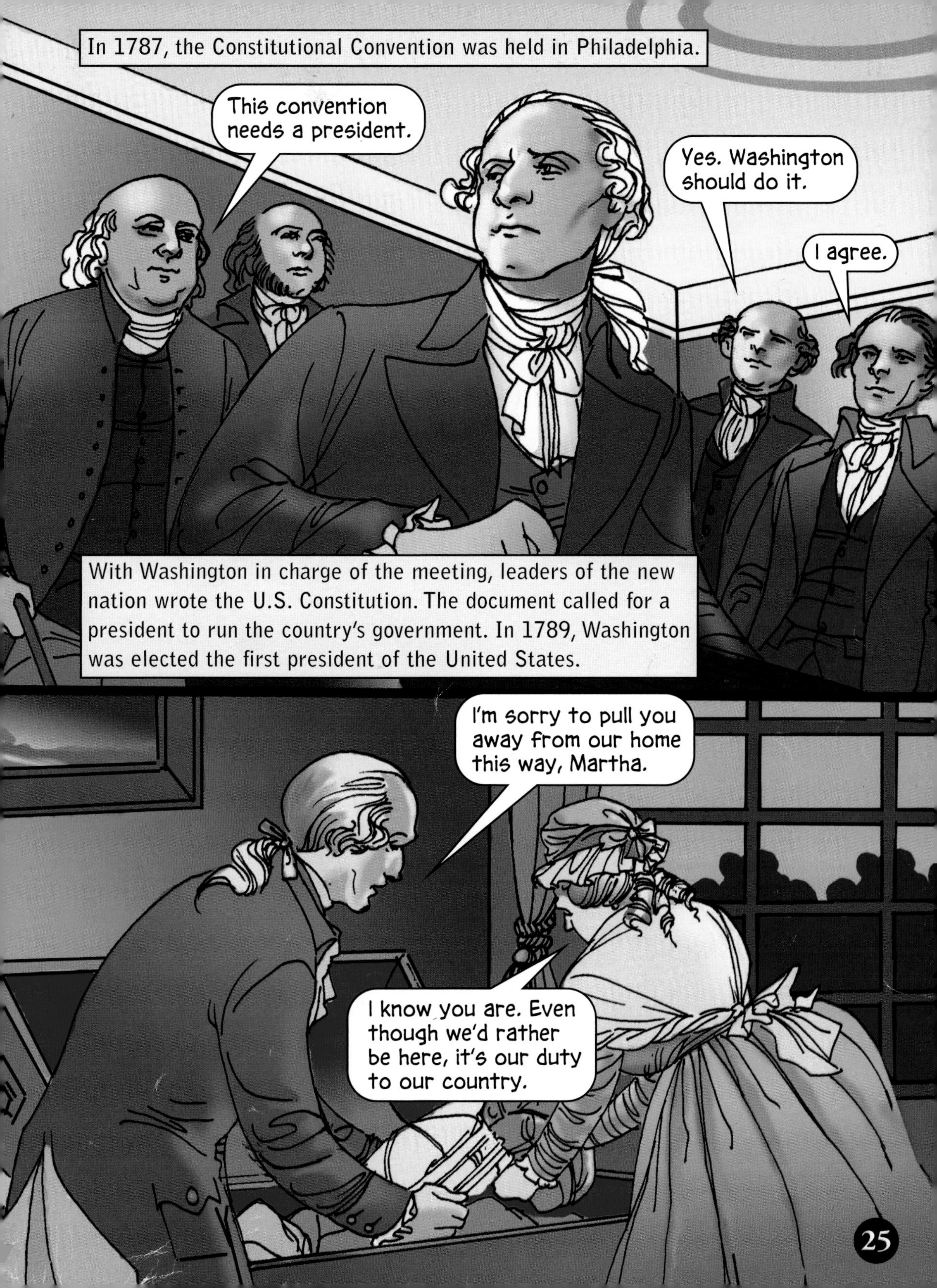
In 1787, the Constitutional Convention was held in Philadelphia.
This convention needs a president.
Yes. Washington should do it.
I agree.
With Washington in charge of the meeting, leaders of the new nation wrote the U.S. Constitution. The document called for a president to run the country's government. In 1789, Washington was elected the first president of the United States.
I'm sorry to pull you away from our home this way, Martha.
I know you are. Even though we'd rather be here, it's our duty to our country.

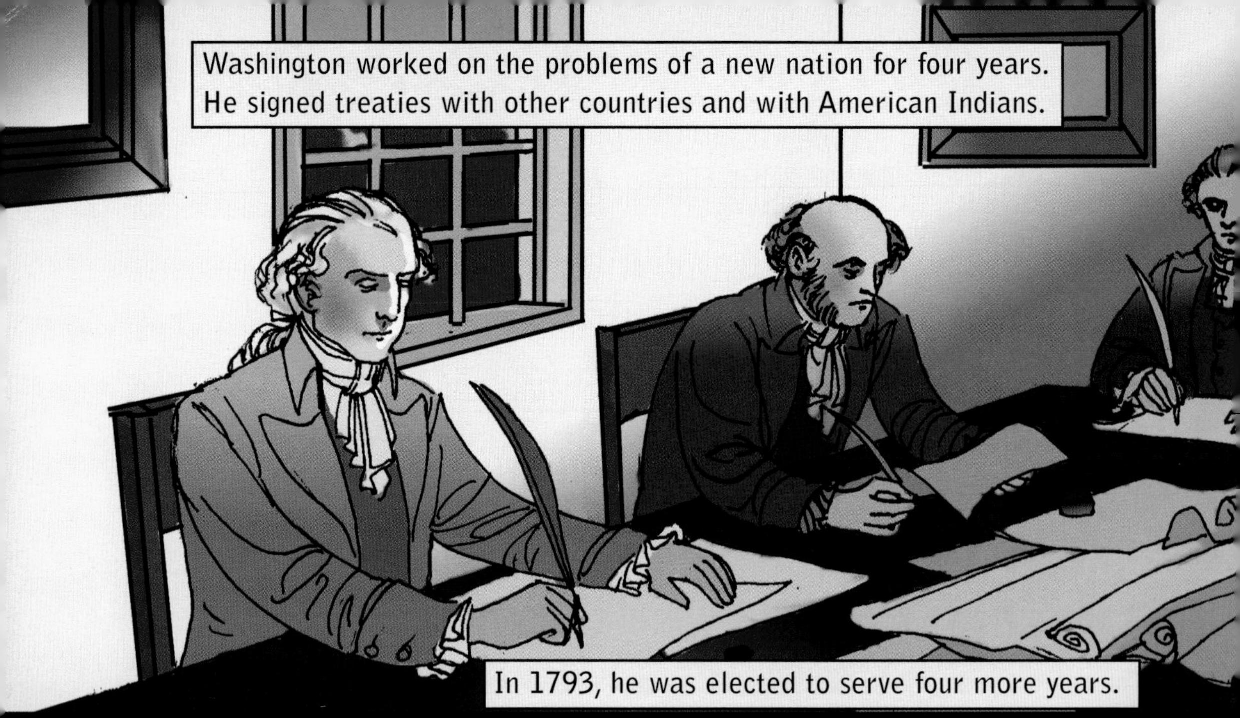
Washington worked on the problems of a new nation for four years. He signed treaties with other countries and with American Indians.
In 1793, he was elected to serve four more years.

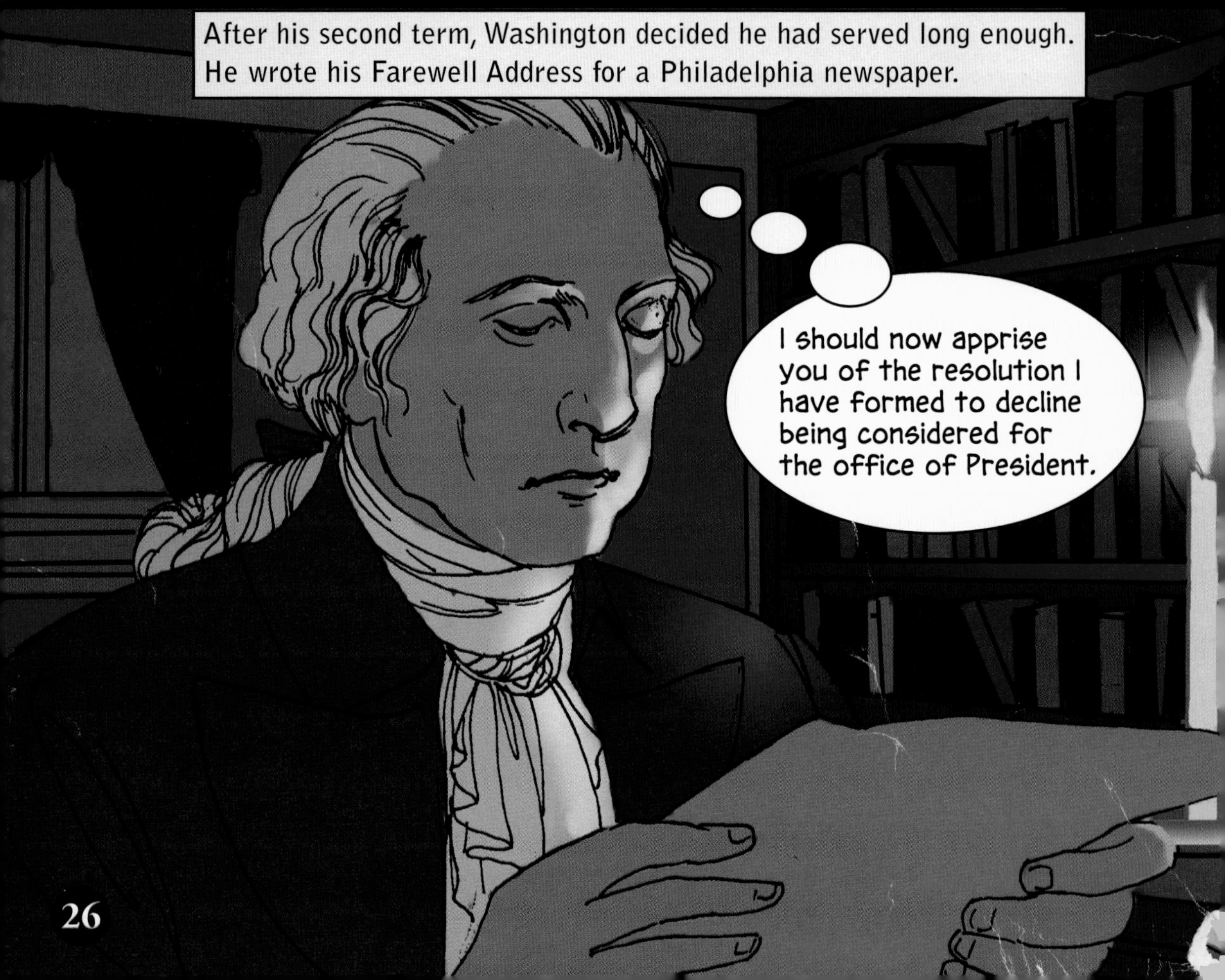
After his second term, Washington decided he had served long enough. He wrote his Farewell Address for a Philadelphia newspaper.
I should now apprise you of the resolution I have formed to decline being considered for the office of President.

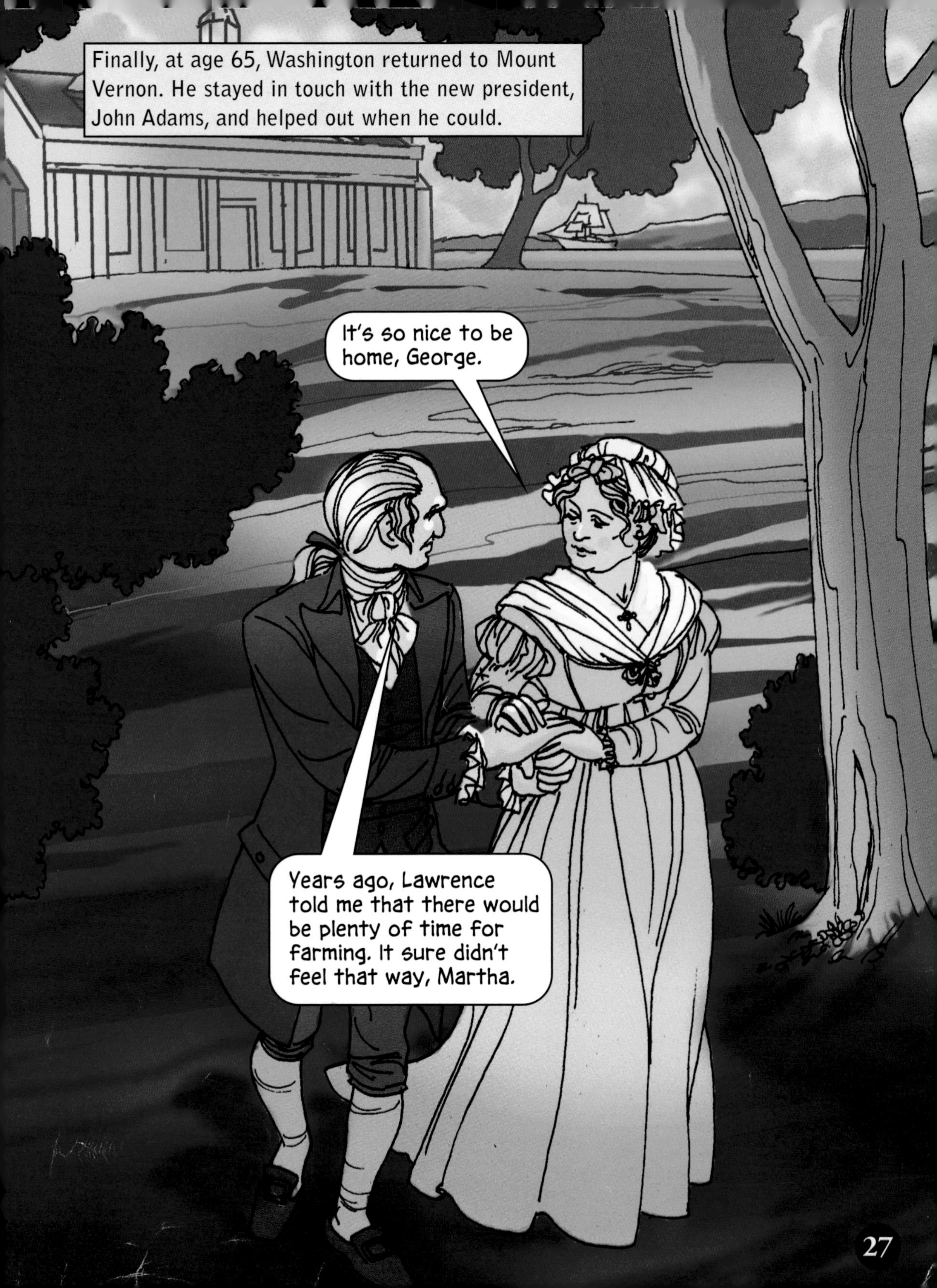
Finally, at age 65, Washington returned to Mount Vernon. He stayed in touch with the new president, John Adams, and helped out when he could.
It's so nice to be home, George.
Years ago, Lawrence told me that there would be plenty of time for farming. It sure didn't feel that way, Martha.

More about
GEORGE WASHINGTON

★ George Washington was born in Westmoreland County, Virginia, February 22, 1732. He was the first of Augustine Washington and Mary Ball's six children.

★ Many tales have been written about Washington. In one story, young Washington chops down his father's cherry tree. When asked if he did it, Washington tells his father the truth. Today, most historians believe this event never happened. They think author Parson Locke Weems created the story to show Washington's honesty.

★ In another tale, Washington throws a silver dollar across the Potomac River. This river is more than 1 mile wide. Still, some people believed Washington was strong enough to do it.

★ During a battle in 1755, Washington had two horses shot out from under him. He also had four bullets pass through his coat.

★ Washington was one of America's largest presidents. He stood more than 6 feet tall, weighed almost 200 pounds, and wore size 13 boots.

★ By the time he was president, Washington had only one tooth left. Many people believe Washington wore false teeth made of wood. Actually, he wore a set made from cow teeth, hippopotamus ivory, and metal springs.

★ Washington suffered from many serious illnesses during his life. He survived malaria, smallpox, typhoid fever, dysentery, and pleurisy.

★ Ice cream was one of Washington's favorite foods. He loved it so much that he installed two ice cream freezers at Mount Vernon.

★ In 1799, Washington came down with a throat infection and never recovered. He died December 14 and was buried at Mount Vernon.

Glossary

constitution (con-stuh-TOO-shuhn)—the system of laws that state the rights of the people and the powers of the government

independence (in-di-PEN-duhnss)—freedom; people who are independent make decisions for themselves.

injustice (in-JUHSS-tiss)—an unfair situation or action

militia (muh-LISH-uh)—a group of civilians who form an army during emergencies

politics (POL-uh-tiks)—the act or science of governing a city, state, or country

Internet Sites

FactHound offers a safe, fun way to find Internet sites related to this book. All of the sites on FactHound have been researched by our staff.

Here's how:

1. *Visit www.facthound.com*
2. Type in this special code **0736849637** for age-appropriate sites. Or enter a search word related to this book for a more general search.
3. Click on the **Fetch It** button.

FactHound will fetch the best sites for you!

READ MORE

Ashby, Ruth. *George and Martha Washington.* Presidents and First Ladies. Milwaukee: World Almanac Library, 2005.

Doeden, Matt. *Winter at Valley Forge.* Graphic History. Mankato, Minn.: Capstone Press, 2006.

Raatma, Lucia. *The Battles of Lexington and Concord.* We the People. Minneapolis: Compass Point Books, 2004.

Roberts, Jeremy. *George Washington.* Presidential Leaders. Minneapolis: Lerner, 2004.

Rosen, Daniel. *Independence Now: The American Revolution, 1763–1783.* Crossroads America. Washington, DC: National Geographic, 2004.

BIBLIOGRAPHY

Ellis, Joseph J. *His Excellency: George Washington.* New York: Alfred A. Knopf, 2004.

Flexner, James Thomas. *George Washington: Anguish and Farewell (1793–1799).* Boston: Little, Brown, 1972.

The Papers of George Washington, University of Virginia. http://gwpapers.virginia.edu/index.html.

Index